JORDAN
PUSHED TO THE LIMIT

Katie Price is Jordan, one of the UK's top celebrities. She is an ex-glamour model, TV presenter, mother and wife. She currently lives in Sussex with husband Peter Andre and her two sons and daughter.

Praise for Katie Price

'I read [Katie Price's books] with pleasure. They are readable tales of lust and rejected love. She is a new kind of star, a bright comet.' Fay Weldon, *Sunday Times Style*

'*Jordan: Pushed to the Limit* is the best book you'll read this year. It's full of page after page of shocking revelations. It's gripping, emotional and amazing. We guarantee you'll read it in one go.' *more*

'Katie is a Cinderella for modern times.' *Grazia*

'What people love about Katie is the fact that she is *so* honest and open about everything. That's what makes her so endearing.'
Kate Garraway, *new!*

'Riveting, honest and heartwarming.' *Woman*

'With Jordan's honest, no nonsense attitude evident on every page, this is a truly compelling read . . . this latest look at her life makes for seriously juicy reading.' *heat*

'Intimate, riveting confessions show her in an unexpected and moving light . . . It's a full-on passionate love story.' *Daily Mail*

'A real page-turner.' *OK!*

'A revealing romp that you'll find hard to put down.' *Star*

Also available by Katie Price

Non-Fiction
Being Jordan
Jordan: A Whole New World

Fiction
Angel
Crystal
Angel Uncovered

Children's Non-Fiction
Katie Price's Perfect Ponies: My Pony Care Book

Children's Fiction
Katie Price's Perfect Ponies
Here Comes the Bride
Little Treasures
Fancy Dress Ponies
Pony Club Weekend
The New Best Friend
Ponies to the Rescue
Star Ponies
Pony 'n' Pooch
Pony in Disguise

Katie Price's Mermaids and Pirates
Follow the Fish
Telescope Overboard
Time for a Picnic
Let's Play I Spy
A Sunny Day
Let's Build a Sandcastle

JORDAN

PUSHED TO THE LIMIT

Katie Price

arrow books

Published in the United Kingdom by Arrow Books in 2009

3 5 7 9 10 8 6 4 2

First published in the United kingdom in 2008 by Century

Arrow Books
Random House, 20 Vauxhall Bridge Road,
London SW1V 2SA

www.rbooks.co.uk

Addresses for companies within The Random House Group Limited can be
found at: www.randomhouse.co.uk/offices.htm

The Random House Group Limited Reg. No. 954009

A CIP catalogue record for this book
is available from the British Library

ISBN 9780099510208

The Random House Group Limited supports The Forest Stewardship
Council (FSC), the leading international forest certification organisation.
All our titles that are printed on Greenpeace approved FSC certified paper
carry the FSC logo. Our paper procurement policy can be found at
www.rbooks.co.uk/environment

Typeset by SX Composing DTP, Rayleigh, Essex
Printed by CPI Bookmarque Ltd, Croydon CR0 4TD

To Pete, Harvey, Junior and Princess, Mum,
Paul, Daniel and Sophie.

CONTENTS

Chapter One: How Did I Get Here?   1

Chapter Two: Breaking Point   17

Chapter Three: The Road to Recovery   37

Chapter Four: Under Threat   51

Chapter Five: Goodbye Nan   62

Chapter Six: My Miscarriage   76

Chapter Seven: Harvey's Progress   99

Chapter Eight: Anniversary   118

Chapter Nine: A Dream Come True?   127

Chapter Ten: Girls Just Wanna Have Fun   164

Chapter Eleven: Katie Price Means
                  Business   177

Chapter Twelve: The Day I Will Never
Forget   193

Chapter Thirteen: Stateside   228

Chapter Fourteen: Please Get Better   252

Chapter Fifteen: Countdown to the Birth   276

Chapter Sixteen: Chaos and Crystal   295

Chapter Seventeen: Our Princess!   312

Chapter Eighteen: The Girl is Back   337

CHAPTER ONE

HOW DID I GET HERE?

I crept into my son Junior's bedroom and watched him sleeping in his cot for a few minutes. He looked so cute, dressed in his blue baby gro. 'Night, Junior,' I whispered. 'Love you so much, promise.' Then I tiptoed out of the room. Tomorrow would be his first Christmas and I wanted to make it extra special for him. But as I thought about the day ahead – thought about seeing my family and friends and having to pretend that I was fine, I had such a knot in my stomach. Instead of looking forward to Christmas Day, I was dreading it. All I wanted to do was shut myself in my bedroom and be alone. I couldn't understand why I felt like this. I was married to the man of my dreams, I had two beautiful children and my career was going from strength to strength – what was wrong with me? Inside I was such a mess. I put on a brave face to everyone, but the truth was, even though Junior was seven months old, I still felt I hadn't bonded with him and I didn't know why. I felt like I was the worst mother in the world. I felt like I was going mad.

Looking back, I know I wasn't the bad mother I thought I was. I know I wasn't mad – I was ill. I had Postnatal Depression. I'd been suffering from it since Junior's birth. But, in December 2005, I had no idea why I felt so out of control and I couldn't tell anyone how I felt, not even Pete, though I think he realised there was something wrong. I wasn't myself; I wasn't the happy, confident girl he had fallen in love with. I didn't want to be around people. I was short-tempered, biting back at anyone whenever they tried to say anything to me; I was stressed, anxious, on edge. I had no confidence. I cried more than I ever had in my life. Worst of all, I felt I couldn't tell anyone about how I felt because I was so ashamed of my feelings. Why couldn't I bond with Junior? What was wrong with me? I knew I loved him, so why couldn't I show it? I kept thinking that I would get better. But I didn't, I seemed to feel worse every day. It's so painful just to remember how it was – it was such a grim, horrible time. I've had to deal with some tough things in the past – like when I was told that Harvey was visually impaired – but I was able to cope with them because I was myself, I was feeling strong and I was well. The Postnatal Depression was one of the worst times of my life, because I felt so confused, so lost. I didn't know why I was feeling so out of control. And what I can't understand is how I came to suffer from it at a time in my life when I had everything I had ever wanted. It just goes to show that it's an illness, and it can happen to anyone. I wouldn't wish it on my worst enemy.

* * *

Junior was born on 13 June 2005, just a year and half after I'd met and fallen instantly, madly, head-over-heels in love with Peter. It will be interesting when we explain to him and his sister that we first met in the Australian jungle on the TV reality show *I'm a Celebrity, Get Me Out of Here!* that's for sure. We've actually kept all the tapes of the shows and the cuttings in a wooden box in the loft, so maybe one day they'll discover it and find out about our unusual love story. Pete and me were caught up in a whirl-wind romance within a week of him arriving in the UK and just three weeks after we'd met, he moved into my house. I couldn't have been happier when I found out I was pregnant, even though we hadn't even been together a year. We weren't married at that time either and, while I wish we had tied the knot before we had the baby, I don't regret it. I knew practically from the first moment I met Pete that he was *the one* and he felt the same about me. We both felt that having children together would complete us as a couple and as a family.

On the whole, my pregnancy with Junior had been okay, apart from the extreme morning sickness. It was great to have Pete to share the experience with – having him by my side at the scans, sharing the excitement and reassuring me when I got anxious about the baby's health – as I'd had no one except my family when I was pregnant with Harvey. I had split up with Harvey's father, Dwight Yorke, shortly after I discovered I was pregnant, and it was very hard dealing with the thought that I was going to be a single parent. I did try and involve him – I always told him about the scans to give him the opportunity to come along, but he never turned up. I think it's important that you always leave the door open for the father to be involved, though, so that they can never throw it back in your face and accuse you of keeping them away from their child.

But towards the end of my pregnancy with Junior, the doctor discovered a complication. There was an unusual membrane above my cervix, which made a natural delivery impossible, and so I ended up having to have a caesarean. Because my pregnancy had caused me to be anaemic, I lost far more blood than is normal during the operation. It was so extreme that the doctors wanted me to have a blood transfusion, something I resisted. Instead, they ordered me to have complete rest and make sure I ate an iron-rich diet. I felt incredibly weak for ages after the birth, and while I ate well, I didn't rest. I was under pressure to lose weight, as I was recording my own fitness DVD at the end of August – barely three months after Junior was born – and then, on 1 September, Pete and me were getting married in a full-on fairy-tale-style wedding. It was too much, too soon after having a baby – I know that now. I pushed myself too far.

From day one, I didn't feel that I had bonded with Junior. I remembered so clearly my feelings for Harvey when he was born, how I felt such intense love when I looked at him, how I wanted to hold him all the time – I never even wanted to put him down in his crib, because I wanted to treasure every minute with him in my arms – how I loved looking after him, feeding him, bathing him, making him smell nice and dressing him in his baby gros. But, with Junior, I just didn't feel like that – I felt exhausted and stressed. I had hired a maternity nurse so I could sleep at night, because I was going back to work in just a couple of weeks and I had also invited Pete's family to stay with us straight after the birth and I felt overwhelmed surrounded by so many people. All I wanted to do was lie on my bed with Junior and Pete beside me, but I felt I couldn't, as I knew how much Pete's family wanted to see the baby. So, instead of resting, I got up and let them see Junior. As the depression took hold of me, I felt that everyone around me was trying to keep me away from Junior, that they were trying to stop me from bonding with him. I was being completely irrational, of course; I couldn't see that they were only trying to help. It was all so different from when I had Harvey, when it was just the two of us and I was the only one looking after him. And I hated the fact that Junior would fall asleep on Pete or on the maternity nurse but not me. It was as if I didn't have the touch with my own son, as if he sensed my feelings.

Of course, everyone wanted to hold Junior and I'd say, 'Yeah, that's fine,' but I really didn't want them to and inside I would be raging, *Go on, then! You take him! You enjoy holding him! You're not letting me bond with my son!* I was a right psycho woman. Everyone was grating on me – my family, Pete's family, Pete – and I took it out on everyone close to me. I felt out of control, as if I had a gremlin of anger building up inside me and at any moment I would explode and tell everyone to fuck off!

To top it all, between Junior's birth and the wedding, Harvey was seriously ill and had to stay in hospital for six weeks, which was the longest time he has ever been away from me. The doctors told us that it was extremely dangerous for him to weigh so much. He was only three years old and yet he weighed over five and a half stone – the average weight of an eleven-year-old. His weight was putting a severe strain on his heart and lungs. It was potentially fatal, as he could have a heart attack. As usual, I'd put on a brave face and pretended to be fine, knowing that I had to be strong for Harvey, but inside I was desperately worried about him and I missed having him at home with me so badly. At this time, I was also back at work, fitting my hectic schedule around hospital visits. I wanted to say to everyone I was working with 'Please take it easy with me, I'm struggling,' but I didn't. I'm sure they would have been sympathetic, but I thought I could get through it on my own. The longer it went on, though, the more depressed I felt.

All this really seemed to come to a head that December, as so many things were getting on top of me, and instead of Junior's first Christmas being the perfect day that I had hoped for, it was awful, because of my depression. We were staying at my mum's house, along with my stepdad Paul, my sister Sophie, my brother Daniel and his wife Louise, my nan, Pete's brother Mike, and Louise (one of my mum's closest friends) and her daughter Rhia, and everyone else was having such a good time. Anyway, at Christmas, no one opens any presents until we're all together – it's one of the Price family traditions. One at a time we each open a present while everyone watches. Usually, it's a tradition that I love, but this time I felt like an outsider. Situations where there are lots of people are also always difficult for Harvey, as he is extremely sensitive to noise. He hated the sound of the paper being ripped off the presents and cried, which wound me up even more and I wanted to shout at everyone to 'Just hurry up and open them!' But Pete and me had bought each other so many presents that we were still opening them long after everyone else had finished unwrapping theirs and they all had to sit there watching us. To be honest, I actually got bored of opening my presents, even though he'd bought me lovely things – a stunning Chopard heart ring, clothes, shoes, make-up, toiletries, more jewellery and helicopter lessons. Much as I was touched by his gifts, the only thing I really wanted was to feel better. At one point, Junior cried because he was tired and needed his nap and I thought *Oh God, do I have to get up and deal with him?* I didn't know why I felt so negative. I never felt like this about Harvey when he was a baby. I watched as Pete went over and picked him up and cuddled him, as always the loving dad. He is such a fantastic dad, I couldn't ask for a better father for my children. Whereas some men might find it hard to express their emotions openly, Pete is always so loving, always hugging and kissing the children, and what's also wonderful is how he treats Harvey and Junior equally. But, back then, seeing Pete show so much love to Junior made me feel jealous, because something was stopping me from giving my son that same love. More than anything else in the world, I wanted to show Junior that I loved him, but I just couldn't. And yet my bond with Harvey hadn't been affected by my depression, and that's what must have made it obvious to Pete that there was something very wrong, because I didn't treat Junior the same way. It hurts now to say it, and it hurts to remember it – it's something that I'll always feel guilty about.

* * *

I had so wanted Christmas to go well. December had already been a stressful month, because I'd come face to face with one of Pete's exes at my best friends' wedding, of all places . . . Gary Cockerill, my make-up artist, and Phil Turner, the DIY makeover TV presenter, got married four days before Christmas and I was so proud that theirs was one of the country's first gay weddings. They really are our best friends. Gary has been doing my make-up since I started out as a glamour model, twelve years ago. We all get on so well and spend loads of time together and it's so comfortable between us that, if we're sitting down in the lounge together, you don't feel that you have to talk – a sign of true friendship, I think. So I was really looking forward to their wedding. I was going to be one of the bridesmaids, along with Francine Lewis, Emma B, Emma Noble and Melinda Messenger, and I'd lined up a beautiful dress to wear – a strapless, figure-hugging white number decorated with Swarovski crystals – though, of course, not as many as I had on my own wedding dress. But then I found out that one of Pete's exes was going to be there – Jackie, the sister of the model and actress Rachel Hunter. Pete had met her in the States just after his breakdown, and he believes she really helped him at a very difficult time, as she introduced him to the therapist Pete saw for over a year. I know I should be glad that Jackie was there for Pete, because from what he's told me about that time he really hit rock bottom – he was suffering twenty to thirty panic attacks a day, and he'd had several psychotic attacks, where he'd seen horrible flashes of violence in his mind, and even ended up spending two weeks in a psychiatric hospital in New York – but my depression had made me feel so vulnerable that I really wasn't up to seeing a woman Pete had been involved with. It wasn't that I was jealous and it wasn't that I thought Pete would be unfaithful, I just felt too low to deal with the situation. As soon as I found out, I said to Pete, 'Don't you dare go up and talk to her, because that will make me feel really shit.' He said that he wouldn't and that I should stop being so paranoid. I tried to push the thought that she was going to be there out of my mind, but I couldn't help feeling tense and anxious.

The wedding was held in the ballroom of the Grosvenor House Hotel on Park Lane and Gary and Phil had gone for an amazing winter wonderland theme, with lots of white and silver, twinkling lights and white mist that swirled around the room – I love these over-the-top weddings! And the boys looked gorgeous in their outfits. As they walked up the aisle, Pete sang one of their favourite songs 'Love's In Need of Love', by Stevie Wonder, and I was so proud of him and so happy for my friends. Gary is such a sweet guy that he'd even done my make-up on his own wedding day – he did Barbara Windsor's as well. I sensed that the other bridesmaids were feeling a bit put out that he didn't do theirs and they probably thought he was favouring me, but then we are best friends. Even though he did his usual amazing job, though, and my hair looked great and my dress was stunning, I felt deeply insecure about how I looked. And that insecurity wasn't helped when, just as I was sipping champagne and chatting to my old agent, Samantha Bond, I turned round and saw Pete talking to Jackie and Rachel. I also had an issue with Rachel Hunter going back to the time I was seeing Dwight Yorke and she had flirted with him behind my back at the Laureus World Sports Awards in Monte Carlo. And *the Pricey* never forgets . . . Immediately, my blood boiled. No way could I just stand there and watch Pete chatting away to the pair of them, so I went over as well. 'Oh, so you *are* saying hello, are you?' I said sarcastically. Pete didn't even attempt to introduce me, so I quickly turned round and marched back to Samantha. When Pete came over, I was really offish with him and the atmosphere was pretty frosty between us, to say the least. I remember chatting to two of my friends from Liberty X, asking them how they would feel in my situation, and whether they would put up with it, and they both agreed it would have pissed them off as well. I know I went on and on about it, and I must have been driving everyone mad, but it was the depression blowing everything out of proportion for me and making me feel that I couldn't cope. If I hadn't been depressed, I could have handled it in my Pricey way and I'd have got it out of my system there and then and not let it eat away inside me. I'd have gone up to Jackie and Pete and said 'Aren't you going to introduce me to her, then? I know what you two got up to.' And then I would have had my say with Rachel: 'I don't know why you're standing there looking so smug when I know you were flirting with Dwight behind my back that time.' But this time, thanks to the Postnatal Depression, I wasn't strong enough to do something as bold as that.

I was fine during the meal, though, because Pete and I were sitting with Gary and Phil and I had my back to Jackie and Rachel. As there was no way I wanted to spoil Gary and Phil's big day, I put on an act that everything was fine, but I was like an eagle keeping my eye on Pete. I didn't even want him to look at Jackie. It's not very nice having to be in the same room as someone your other half has gone out with. Pete and I have always had an agreement that we would never put each other in that situation, but, of course, we had no choice on this occasion, as it was our friends' wedding. I'd told Gary about it when I found out Jackie was invited, but I could hardly turn round and say he couldn't ask her because of me. It's not my fault that Pete's had so many women, so many that he's lost count, but I've had to see them on his music videos, at family weddings, at restaurants, on planes and now at the wedding of my closest friends.

*   *   *

Gary and Phil's wedding reminded me of my own wedding day, reminded me only too well of how it hadn't been the perfect day I had dreamt of. I couldn't have been happier that I was marrying Pete, and everything about the day – my incredible dress, the amazing marquee and entertainment – had all more than matched my expectations, but my depression had taken the shine off everything; I hadn't been myself at all. I'd also had a problem with the photographer taking so many posed pictures and making the day feel like work. Plus, I ended up with hardly any pictures of me with my family. The only part I enjoyed was walking up the aisle and saying my vows with Pete – that memory I treasure, as it was perfect. But, from then on, I'd felt tense and stressed out, and remembering that made me feel even sadder, made me feel even more of a failure. The night of Gary and Phil's wedding I lay in bed, unable to sleep. I just didn't know how much longer I could go on feeling like this.

CHAPTER TWO

BREAKING POINT

With Christmas behind me, I still wasn't looking forward to the year ahead. In fact, I was absolutely dreading it. My depression was casting a shadow over everything. I'd only been married four months, but my marriage was being put under severe pressure by how I was feeling and acting. It's no exaggeration to say that Pete and me came close to splitting up at that time. It wasn't because I had stopped loving him – I still loved him more than anything – but because

I was so desperately unhappy and moody. And our sex life, which until now had been fantastic, hit an all-time low. I just didn't feel like it, not one little bit, and that was unheard of for me. It was nothing to do with Pete, as I still thought he was gorgeous and fancied him like mad, I just didn't want to have sex; I had no urge at all in my body to want it. My sex drive had first deserted me during my pregnancy and I had promised Pete that, when I'd recovered from the birth, I'd be back to myself, back to wanting to make love with him. But it didn't happen. Whenever he suggested we have sex, I'd say, 'No, I don't want to.' And then, because I didn't want him to feel rejected, I'd add, 'It's nothing to do with you, it's me. I don't know what the matter is with me.' He kept saying, 'That's fine, I understand.' But then he'd blow it by making a sexy gesture or by saying he was really horny. And I would want to say, '*Well, go and have a wank, then, because I'm not doing anything!*' And it used to really get my back up whenever he mentioned wanting sex. I didn't think I should have to force myself to do it just because he wanted it. But I missed the intimacy of making love with Pete, missed that closeness it brings. I just wanted him to hold me and cuddle me, but it was hard because of my illness. He was still there for me and he'd still do anything for me, but he said he was scared to say anything, because he didn't know how I'd react – all too often I'd snap back and be foul. All I wanted was to be close to him, but the depression was making me push him away.

Work, which had always been my escape, was stressing me out as well. I'd been doing lots of shoots for *OK!* and having meetings about my jewellery and lingerie range and music career, and I was having a hard time holding it together. Usually, I loved my work, but at the moment everything was getting to me. During this period, I opened the Guess store in the Bluewater shopping centre in Kent. As I got ready for the event, I thought *I hope I look thin*. Yes, I had lost weight, but after Junior was born, I never felt I'd got my figure back. I think that, even if you are the weight you want to be, you're never happy when you reach it, you just want to lose more. Now, when I look back at the pictures of me that December, I think *God, I really was thin, too thin probably*. I wore a short denim skirt and a little Guess top. But I didn't feel good about myself. Worse, I found it really hard being surrounded by people and I really didn't like anyone approaching me, wanting autographs and pictures. After I'd opened the store, Pete, his parents and me wandered round the whole centre. I wanted to do a bit of shopping, but people kept coming up to me and I couldn't concentrate. The noise of the crowds seemed louder than usual and I wanted to shout: 'Stop staring at me, just fuck off and let me be normal for a day!' It was too much; I was agitated, stressed and had no patience – which was so unlike me. If I could barely handle one afternoon with the crowds, how the hell was I going to cope in a few weeks' time when I was going to be promoting my fitness DVD and second autobiography? In the past, I would have been excited by the challenge of so much work and I'd have loved meeting my fans, but now I was dreading it.

I had put myself under unnecessary pressure and said yes to making the fitness DVD, even though I knew it was too soon after Junior's birth. I was so run down after his birth – I'd lost so much blood, and I'd gone on a diet too quickly. My body needed more time to recover. I never should have gone ahead with it at that time – never, never, never. I always used to think that I had to prove myself, that I had to take on all the work I was offered, worrying that, if I didn't, I might not get offered anything again. I'm self-employed and I know my work could end at any moment – that's where the fear comes from. And I suppose I like to prove to people that you can have kids and still work, but I've now learnt to admit when enough is enough, and you can only do what your body lets you. I hadn't listened to mine and I was paying the price.

And now, in January 2006, I had to promote the DVD. I had a packed schedule of press, TV and radio interviews, shoots and signings all over the country. And I was feeling worse and worse – I didn't want to be around people at all. The only way I can describe how I felt was that it was like someone was crushing my head with a steel band and I wanted to scream. I didn't want to talk to anyone, I didn't want to see anyone and I didn't want anyone round the house. But I was trying to soldier on, so no one around me had any idea how bad I felt. I wanted to cry and beg them to help me, tell them that I wasn't well, but then I'd think *I can't, I have to be strong*, because I didn't want anyone to think that I was a bad mum.

Somehow I managed to get through the DVD promotion, but I knew I had the book launch coming up with more interviews and signings and I seriously didn't think I could cope. What made it harder was that I had already talked about my worries about not bonding with Junior in my autobiography and I knew that journalists were bound to ask me about my feelings for my son now. Sure enough, they did, and I found it so difficult, because I still didn't feel better. I was so raw with emotion. So I pretended that I was fine, because it was too painful to admit the truth. I actually took Junior with me to quite a few of the signings and interviews, because I really wanted to be with him, and everyone would say 'Oh he's so gorgeous!'. But instead of enjoying their compliments, I'd be thinking *Don't touch him! Keep away from my baby!*

I felt as if I couldn't escape from these negative feelings. Before I met Pete, if I'd been feeling low my solution would have been to go out clubbing and to get pissed. I know that doesn't solve anything, but at least for a few hours I could have had a break from my state of mind. When I split up with Dane Bowers all those years ago, I remember going out clubbing and drinking to numb the pain and now I needed something to take me out of my head in that same way. But Pete hates clubs and hates me drinking, so I knew I couldn't take that route. I was feeling more and more desperate – I didn't know how much longer I could go on pretending that everything was fine. One night at the beginning of February, when I was in the middle of my book promotion tour, I reached rock bottom. Pete was working on some songs in the studio and I went upstairs to my dressing room, telling him that I wanted to try on some of my outfits to see what looked good for my interviews. Once the door was safely shut, I sat down at my dressing table, staring numbly at my reflection. What was happening to me? I couldn't bear to feel like this anymore. Slowly I reached for my bag and opened it. My fingers touched a small package and I pulled it out and looked at it for a few minutes, hesitating – did I really want to do this? A few days earlier, I'd texted an old friend of mine from my clubbing days and asked him to get me something, anything that would give me a buzz. And here it was in my hand. Maybe this would help? I was so desperate that I had to do something. Looking back, I'm so ashamed of what happened next, and it affected Pete so deeply that I don't want to say what drug I took; it's enough to say that I took something that, from what people had told me, was supposed to give you a high. I think I knew then that there was something seriously wrong with me, because I was just upstairs in my house, and yet I was desperate to get out of my head — it wasn't as if I was out partying with friends, I was alone. After I'd taken it, I thought, *This feels good*, and I took some more. Because I'm naïve about drugs, as I've never been into them, I had no idea how much I should be taking. And, suddenly, I started to feel really strange, my heart seemed to be racing fast, I felt hot and I began to panic. *Oh my God, had I overdosed? Was I going to die?*

Trying to pull myself together, I quickly went back downstairs and joined Pete in the studio, trying to act as if everything was normal, when all the time I was thinking, *Fuck, what have I done to myself?* Eventually, we went to bed but sleep was out of the question as I lay there wide awake, tormenting myself with my thoughts, convinced that I was going to die. My heart still seemed to be racing wildly and I felt weak and shaky. Pete could obviously tell that there was something wrong, because he kept asking me if I was all right. I lied and told him that I was. I knew there was no way that I could tell him the truth. Pete had already told me that the one thing he's dead against is drugs. He said the only reasons he'd divorce me were if I were unfaithful or I'd taken drugs, so I had to pretend and I kept trying to tell myself that in a minute I would feel okay, that I'd calm down. But I didn't, and I was getting more and more freaked. The feeling of panic and the racing sensation of my heart seemed to be getting worse.

Finally I cracked, 'Pete, will you please call me a doctor? I really don't feel well.' Tears were welling up in my eyes as I went on, 'I think I'm going to die.'

Pete was horrified, 'What's the matter?' he exclaimed, as he took me in his arms, trying to reassure me and calm me down. I realised, with a feeling of dread, that I was going to have to come clean with him, even though I knew what the consequences would be, but that's how convinced I was that I was going to die.

'Pete, I've got something to tell you.' I couldn't stop myself from crying. 'I know you'll divorce me, but I have to tell you, I have to be honest.' Pete looked stunned, but I carried on, 'I've just taken some drugs.'

Straightaway he pulled away from me and leapt out of bed as if he'd been hit.

'You what!' he shouted. 'My God, that's it, that's the end of us!'

'Please Pete,' I begged him, but he wouldn't listen.

'You're fucking stupid. That's it! I'm sorry, Kate. I'll stay with you until you're feeling better, but then I'm going.'

I stretched out my arms and pleaded with him to come back to me, but he wouldn't, he just stood there looking absolutely shell-shocked. I felt as if I was on a different planet, thinking *That's it, I've just destroyed my marriage.*

The doctor arrived quickly – he lived on the same private estate as us, so he was with us in about ten minutes. As relieved as I was to see him, I was also deeply embarrassed and ashamed. He's looked after Harvey and Junior when they've been ill in the past and I thought *Oh my God, he's going to think I'm not a good mum because I've done this and that I'm mad.* When he asked me what the matter was, I had to admit it – 'I'm really sorry I've taken some drugs.' But he was completely non-judgmental and simply questioned me about what I'd taken and how much before taking my blood pressure. Finally, he told me that I was going to be okay, that I definitely wasn't going to die. And, by then, I was starting to feel better. He left shortly after that and the row between Pete and me kicked off even worse than before.

'I'm really sorry, Pete. This was a one-off, it will never happen again. Please don't leave me,' I begged him.

'I'm sorry, Kate, but I am. You've been biting at me, you haven't been yourself for ages and now you've gone and done this and you know how I feel about drugs. You're going to be an unfit mother and I can't be around you. I'm taking Junior.'

'You're not fucking taking my child!' I screamed back at him. And even in the middle of what felt like my heart breaking, I thought *I know I'm not a bad mum, I love my kids. I'm not well, there's something wrong with me.*

The row went on and on and then, around two o'clock in the morning, I just lost it. I raced out of the house screaming, 'If you don't want me, I'm going and I'm never coming back!' I was in a terrible state, crying hysterically, but somehow I managed to get in my car and drive away. I had no idea what I was doing or where I was going. As it happens, I only got as far as the bottom of the road to the nursery where Harvey went, so I pulled into the car park and sat there, completely distraught, confused and desperate. *Oh my God, I'm not going to have Pete anymore. What am I going to do? I've ruined everything. I can't live without him.* And I seriously thought, *Shall I just end it now? Drive into this wall and kill myself and then no one will have to worry about me anymore? What is wrong with me? . . . What the hell are you thinking of? You can't do this to the kids, to Pete, to your mum. You're stronger than this. Pull yourself together.* But then again came the thought that I just couldn't go on without Pete. And because I was so ashamed of taking drugs, *How am I going to explain to people why we're not together and what a dirty thing I've done?* Finally, I somehow managed to pull myself together enough to drive home. I knew I wasn't a druggie – I'd taken drugs as a cry for help, I was ill. I had to go back and see Pete and face the consequences. As soon as I walked through the door, Pete said, 'I'm going to have to get your mum over here to look after you, because I can't.'

'Don't you dare!' I screamed back. No way did I want my mum to know what I had done, because I felt so ashamed of taking drugs; that's not how she'd brought me up. And I knew she'd be hurt that I hadn't been able to tell her how I'd been feeling. But even though it was after three o'clock, Pete went ahead and called her, and as he told her what had happened, I kept trying to grab the phone off him and shouting at her, 'Don't you even think about coming here!' I really was beside myself.

'I am,' she insisted. 'Someone needs to sort you out.'

Twenty minutes later, she arrived and at first I wouldn't open the door to her, but Pete let her in, saying, 'I can't have your mum locked outside.' So there we all were sitting round the kitchen table and there was no more putting on a brave face anymore, no more pretending that I was fine.

I took a deep breath, I had to be completely honest now.

'I have got a problem. I'm not right, I still don't feel like I've bonded with Junior. I do need help; I do need to see someone. I've kept it all in about how I've been feeling and I haven't told you, but I don't know what

I'm doing anymore. I don't know why I took those drugs, I didn't even want to take them. I just wanted something to pick me up.'

As I spoke, I was looking at Pete, willing him to believe in me, to understand that I was ill.

'Where did you get them from?' Pete asked angrily, and when I told him, he said, 'Right, you're not seeing that person anymore. Give me his number, I'm going to tell him to stay away from you.'

Mum was brilliant and, while Pete and me were shouting, she was completely calm. 'Look, Pete,' she said, 'You've had depression yourself, you've got to help her. She's taken drugs as a cry for help, you can't leave her.'

I've never seen Pete look so angry and upset before. Not only was he furious that I'd taken drugs, but I also think he was deeply hurt that I hadn't confided in him about how I'd been feeling. I was still in a complete state – confused, shocked about what I'd done, praying that Pete wouldn't leave me. I felt as if our marriage was hanging in the balance as Pete struggled with his emotions. Then he decided to call his brother Mike, who he's really close to, and tell him what had happened. When he said that he was going to leave me, to my relief Mike was also great. He told Pete that he couldn't, that this was the time that I needed him more than anything and that he had to stick by me, that we could work through this. Mike is so good; whenever we have a problem, I know he will talk sense into Pete. I have to really thank my mum and Mike for what they said that night, because if it hadn't been for them God knows what would have happened between Pete and me. Mike played a big part in persuading Pete to stay with me, because Pete was so adamant that he was going, but that phone call to Mike helped change his mind. Although Mike had made him think twice about leaving, Pete was still really angry with me. It's not like he suddenly switched into being all lovey-dovey.

'Are there any more drugs in the house?' he demanded, as soon as he finished his call with Mike.

I shook my head and he carried on, 'Well, if I find any, that will be it.'

I swore that there wasn't, thinking, *I'm never doing that again.*

And then he said, 'This is it, Kate. You've got to get help. I can't cope with this anymore. I've got to know that you're going to help yourself.'

'I promise I will, Pete,' I said, and I got up and hugged him, because I couldn't bear the distance between us anymore. 'I will get help,' I told him. 'I want to get better, I don't want to feel like this anymore.'

* * *

'You'll be fine,' Pete reassured me, as I slowly opened the car door and climbed out. It was a cold, grey February afternoon and right now I wanted to be anywhere but here – here being outside The Priory.

'See you later,' I muttered, as I slammed the door and started walking towards the building, feeling sick with nerves. What was I doing here? I couldn't believe I had ended up at a hospital for treating people with mental health problems. I looked over my shoulder, paranoid that I'd be spotted walking in and that people would think I was nuts. But I knew that I urgently needed help and I knew that, if I didn't get it right now, my marriage was quite possibly over.

Although so much was at stake, I couldn't help feeling awkward and embarrassed when I met the doctor for the first time. I knew I had to see him, because I wanted to be with Pete so much and I knew if I didn't prove to Pete that I was trying to help myself that he wouldn't stand for it. I couldn't just rely on Pete to pull me out of this; I had to do it myself. But it was so hard. First of all, I had to tell him all about myself, about how I'd been feeling, and I had to admit about taking drugs a few days earlier. 'I've done something really stupid,' I said, and I couldn't help feeling that he was looking at me like I had a screw loose. I'm sure he wasn't, but that's just how I felt at the time. I have always been so strong and coped with everything life had thrown at me, so why not now? He asked me all these questions – Why had I taken the drugs? Had I done it before? Did I want to do it again? All I wanted to say was *Please help me!* But I found it so hard to talk to him. It was as if I was trying to prove to him that there was nothing wrong with me, when of course there was . . . He kept telling me that I had to open up, that this wasn't an interview; I didn't have to watch what I was saying.

'It's so difficult for me to trust anyone,' I told him. I knew I was holding back and, even though I kept telling myself, *He's a doctor, you can trust him*, I didn't know for sure that I could. I've been ripped off so many times in the past when people promised that I could trust them and then turned round and sold a story on me.

Finally, he told me that he believed I had Postnatal Depression. However, he also thought the depression had been building up for years – something which my GP had also thought, my mum later revealed. She'd called my GP the morning after I'd lost it and taken the drugs to ask him where I could get help and he had referred her to the doctor at The Priory. He told my mum that he'd been expecting something like this to happen to me for a long time, because I'd been through so much, what with bringing up a disabled child, at first as a single parent, and having to cope with his regular stays in hospital, as well as having to deal with my own cancer scare.

The doctor in The Priory went further and asked how I relaxed when I wasn't working, and what came out from that discussion was that I simply didn't unwind. Since I married Pete, my life had changed so much and, yes, I couldn't have been happier to be married to him, but there were some changes that weren't for the best. I had stopped going out and socialising with my friends – I hadn't even seen my oldest friend Clare since before the wedding. I just don't know what had happened to our friendship, it had all fallen apart when she'd met her new boyfriend, who took against me for some reason. My mum had bumped into Clare in Brighton and told her that I was feeling very low, but she had never called to see how I was. So I'd had no one to confide in about just how bad I felt, except Pete and my mum, and, as I didn't want to let them down, I'd tried to be strong for them. And now it had all backfired and here I was, at an all time low.

The doctor recommended I see him every week for therapy, but I didn't think that was going to be enough to pull me out of the depression. 'Please,' I begged him, 'I need you to put me on something, anything, because I just don't think that talking about how I feel is going to help me.' At first he said he didn't want to, but finally he gave in and prescribed a very low dose of anti-depressant. But he said that I had to make sure that I took it every day and not miss a dose, warning me that if I didn't take it regularly, the medication could have side-effects. I had to take 10 mg for the first week and then increase the dose to 20 mg. He also told me that I couldn't suddenly come

35

off the medication, and that he would have to monitor me carefully when I did, as again you can get side-effects and feel dizzy and disoriented.

It was such a relief to finally admit how I'd been feeling and to hear the doctor telling me that I wasn't mad. Not only had the depression put such a strain on my family life, but it had also really affected my work as well. The day after what I now see as my cry for help I was due to be in Dublin for an interview on a TV show to promote my autobiography and I had to pull out. There was no way that I was in any fit state to see anyone, let alone appear on TV and talk about my life. I also had to cancel a number of book signings. I hated letting my fans down, but there was no other way; I just couldn't have done it. When I do my signings, I like to put 100 per cent into it and to chat to people, but at that moment I had nothing to give. Instead, I had to give myself time to get better for my boys' sake and for Pete.

CHAPTER THREE

THE ROAD TO RECOVERY

But it took a long time to recover from Postnatal Depression and sometimes, even now, I don't know if it has ever quite left me. It's something I'm very aware of, something I'm afraid of too, because I never want to feel like that again. And I think I'll always feel guilt and sadness because I didn't bond with Junior straightaway, even though I know I loved him and that it was all because I was ill. Even when my depression was at its worst, I still tried to be a good mum to him. All I can do is put that time behind me and show him all the love now that I felt I couldn't before. I now know that I'm not alone in feeling like I did – I learned that one in every ten mothers suffers from Postnatal Depression. Since my own experience, I've spoken to a few women who've had it, and none of them liked to admit it either, because, like me, they were ashamed of their feelings. They thought they could cope with it themselves and that time would heal. In January 2007, I decided to talk about my experiences on *This Morning*, because I wanted other mothers to know that having Postnatal Depression is nothing to be ashamed of, that it's an illness and that you can get better.

But back to February 2006 . . .

I have to admit that I've always expected instant results, so I was disappointed when I started taking the medication but didn't suddenly feel back to my old self. When I told Pete, he reassured me that it would take a while before the medication took effect. I'm afraid to say that, after a couple of weeks, when I couldn't notice any difference, I upped the dose myself to 30 mg. I shouldn't have done it without consulting the doctor, but I still felt so low and I was desperate to feel better.

Pete was incredibly supportive during this time. He had been through his own breakdown and he understood how I was feeling, but he was also tough with me – 'I'll stick by you 100 per cent, provided you want to help yourself. If I know you want to help yourself and go to see the doctor, then I'll know you're making an effort and I'll stick by you through it. But, if you don't want to and you can't be bothered and you'd rather get your hair and nails done than work through it, then this is going to drive me away.' I knew he meant it and I wasn't going to let him or my boys down (though I still managed to get my hair and nails done, of course . . .). And I had learnt a valuable lesson: I was not going to bottle up my feelings anymore, I was going to tell people – Pete especially – exactly how I felt. I wasn't going to pretend that I was fine. Pretending that I was fine had very nearly destroyed me and I was never going to go down that path again.

But it was a tough time. And while Pete was there for me, he told me that he was very hurt that I hadn't told him about how I was feeling, that instead I'd written about it in my book. Looking back, writing my second autobiography, *A Whole New World*, was a kind of therapy for me, as it's a totally honest account of how I was feeling back then. I know some people might have been hurt by some of the things I said, but all I can say is that that is how I was feeling when I was suffering from Postnatal Depression and that I'm really sorry if it upset anyone I'm close to. Pete also said that I had upset a lot of people by talking about his past – specifically his many exes. But I don't give a shit what they think, I was just pointing out how Pete's past made me feel. Pete was upset, too, that I had talked about his family, because he's so protective of them. But all I said was that I found it hard to be surrounded by people so soon after Junior was born. It was nothing against them at all, because they are lovely, caring people; it was just the depression making me feel like that.

Shortly after my visit to The Priory, Pete's mum and dad came over from Cyprus for a visit. I told them that I was really sorry for the way I had acted just after Junior was born, and I explained that I was suffering from Postnatal Depression and told them how I was on medication now, trying to sort myself out. They were really upset to hear about what I'd been through, and they told Pete that he had to help me and look after me. Those words made me feel so much better; it showed they didn't hate me for how I'd behaved towards them when I was depressed. But while it was good to be able to tell them how I felt, I still hated it when his mum picked up Junior and cuddled him – it brought back too many memories of how I felt just after he was born, how I felt everyone was trying to stop me bonding with my son. But then, as I tried to explain to Pete later, it could have been any woman forming a bond with Junior, it wasn't personal to his mum, and I really hoped that I would stop feeling like this soon.

* * *

In March we went to Disney World in Florida – it was a much-needed break and although we were there to do a shoot for *OK!* it did actually feel like a holiday. We got to hang out lots with the kids and I also fitted in serious amounts of shopping, so a result there, as far as I'm concerned. The shoot itself was fun – I got to dress up in some amazing full-length, full-on dresses and pose with Pete round the park, as if I was a princess and he was my prince. It may sound corny, but I think we deserved a bit of fun after what we'd been through . . . For one set of nighttime shots, they actually closed down the park for us, which was really weird, because it was like being on a film set. It was one o'clock in the morning and there was nobody around except us and the crew and we were posing in Cinderella's coach with the Disney music playing and the fairy-tale castle behind us. It's blue in the pictures I've got, but they can light it any colour and, for a while, they lit it pink just for me!

Posing with Pete in this fairy-tale setting made me think again about how I really wanted to renew my wedding vows with him. That may sound strange to some people, as we haven't been together that long, but I didn't enjoy my wedding day. When I renew my vows I really want to enjoy the day and be in the right frame of mind. I want to celebrate my love for Pete, who has been so amazing and stuck by me and been like my rock through such difficult times. And I think it's important for me and Pete to renew our vows, because boy have we been tested in our relationship . . . We both feel that, because we've been able to get through everything that's happened to us so far – the

Postnatal Depression, the lack of sex – and yet still be strong, we know we can get through anything. Of course, what I didn't know back in March 2006 was how much more Pete and I would have to go through.

* * *

Meanwhile, the medication was starting to have a positive effect on me and I was beginning to feel slightly better, though still not fully myself. But although I had promised Pete that I would see the doctor at The Priory, I didn't, as I hadn't really felt comfortable confiding in him. Pete picked me up on it and told me straight, 'I'm not telling you what to do, but you really should see the doctor. You can't just see him once and expect everything to be okay. I know because I've been there myself.' But before I had chance to arrange another appointment, I found out that I was pregnant again. It was a shock, though we hadn't exactly been careful. I wanted to have more children, but I just wasn't sure that this was the right time, as I knew that I still hadn't got over the Postnatal Depression. As soon as I told Pete, he said, 'Oh my God, I've only just got you back. I don't want to lose you again.'

'I think I feel okay now,' I told him, and I thought I did, but I had a long way to go . . . Although we were both worried about my depression coming back again, Pete and me were both happy about the news, but there was no question about that. We really wanted another baby.

I'd received such good care from the doctors at The Portland, a private hospital in London, when I was pregnant with Junior that I decided I wanted to go there again. When I saw Dr Gibb, my obstetrician, I told him all about my Postnatal Depression and said that I was worried about being on medication while I was pregnant. Immediately he wanted me to see a therapist he worked with who would help me come off the medication and give me help to overcome my depression. He said that I should see her throughout my pregnancy, and I was happy to do this, because I so didn't want the depression to come back. Within a matter of days, I was booked in to see her, and this is where I really feel I started to make progress in my recovery.

From the beginning, I felt more relaxed with Galin. She was older than me, immaculately dressed and she just seemed as if she could have been one of my mum's friends. I felt comfortable with her straight-away and I felt I could trust her and be completely open about my feelings – which is how you need to be if therapy is going to be of any help. She was concerned that I was on such a high dosage of anti-depressants and, when I admitted that I had upped the levels myself, she told me that I really shouldn't have done it, but that she would help me come off the tablets gradually. I told her everything about how my depression had made me feel, how I felt about Junior, about my relationship with Pete, about how I didn't feel like having sex. And she explained that the Postnatal Depression and the high dosage of medication were combining to suppress my sex drive. She also explained how Postnatal Depression is an illness that can be cured, with medication and with therapy. But, just as several other doctors had pointed out, she also agreed that she could see the depression had been building up in me for a while now, because of all the stressful things that had happened to me in the past and how having too many people around me immediately after Junior was born and going back to work too soon had only made it worse.

She also saw Pete, to explain to him why I'd been feeling like I did. She told him that some women can have Postnatal Depression for up to six years and explained to him about the impact of Postnatal Depression and anti-depressants on my sex drive. But then she said to both of us, 'What would you rather do? Take the tablets and get better? Or don't take them and put up with the depression?' The answer was obvious. I didn't ask to have Postnatal Depression. Unfortunately, when you get married you have to put up with some difficult times – for better for worse. But I also knew in my heart that this was a phase and I had confidence that I would get better.

In the months that followed, Galin helped me wean myself off the tablets – first reducing the dose from 30 to 20 mg, then down to 10 mg. There were a couple of days when I forgot to take them at all and I ended up feeling so weird – I had a heady feeling as if everything around me was in slow motion. Gradually, I felt more like myself again. There wasn't a day when I just woke up and suddenly thought I'm better now, but day by day, I began to feel closer to Junior, more able to express my love for him. I started to enjoy my work again and I was happier around people. Two years on, I think I'm almost there, I'm not 100 per cent better, but I'm 99.9 per cent there.

Just as I was feeling slightly better, someone very close to me became seriously ill. It was Essie, my eighty-two-year-old nan, my mum's mum. She had emphysema through years of smoking and had problems breathing as a result. We'd all nagged her for ages about giving up and she'd always say she was cutting down or she'd given up, but she never did. She was like a naughty child and mum was forever going round to her bungalow and discovering the stash of cigarettes she'd hidden away. I was so upset about nan. We're such a close family and my nan has always had a special place in my heart. Mum had to work full time when my brother and me were little and nan was the one who picked us up from school and looked after us till mum finished work. I remember she would always give us a KitKat and *Sons and Daughters* would be on the TV.

My mum reckons that I am like nan in so many ways. We're both complete exhibitionists and Essie was a very impulsive, passionate woman who loved socialising and having a laugh. Apparently, whenever there was any kind of party, in her younger days, she'd be the first to try to take men's trousers down! Way to go, Nan! When she was seventeen, she fell head-over-heels in love with this man called Charlie and she threatened to kill herself if her family didn't allow her to marry him. Well, they gave in, but two years later, when she'd just given birth to a daughter, Charlie said that he'd met someone else and they ended up getting divorced. It must have been tough for her having a baby and being on her own. She was only nineteen and attitudes towards single parents were very different then. Luckily, she found love again with my granddad, Harvey. I love the story of how they met – it's almost as surreal as how I met Pete.

Nan used to do promotion work, and one time she was working for the World Trade Fair in London and she had to pose as a mermaid for one of the exhibits. She had beautiful waist-length auburn hair (that's probably where Princess gets her colouring from) and she had to lie there topless, with just her long hair to preserve her dignity. In front of her was a tank full of fish, and people would pay, look through the tank, and be treated to the spectacle of my nan, the mermaid, reclining and brushing her hair. My granddad was one of the visitors and he was very taken with her. They ended up dating and marrying. Nan was not a mermaid for long, though, she got so bored that one day she lit up a cigarette and ended up getting the sack!

She was always so proud of me for my work. She absolutely loved what I did and nothing shocked her. She'd look at all my glamour shots in the lads mags and tabloids and watch me on TV. The more outrageous I was, the better, as far as she was concerned and I'd always been able to talk to her about everything. She loved hearing about what I'd been up to.

When she went into hospital, I visited her as much as I could. It was heartbreaking seeing her lying there in such an impersonal ward. She just wanted to go home to her bungalow in Hove, and she kept saying, 'Please, just get me home, all I want to do is walk along the seafront with Micky.' Micky was her white poodle and she adored him. Every day she'd take him for a walk by the sea. She knew all the homeless people who hung out down there and she'd sit with them on one of the benches and have a fag.

Everybody in her area knew her and liked her. And now here she was struggling to breathe. It was really, really sad.

It also put other things in perspective. I felt my relationship with Pete was stronger than ever. He had been so good to me when I was suffering from depression, standing by me 100 per cent and helping me get better. When I told him I'd taken drugs that night in February, I was convinced that he was going to divorce me, but it just goes to show that, if you are honest with your partner and you get help, your relationship can get through even the really tough times.

CHAPTER FOUR

UNDER THREAT

Since being in the public eye, I've had my fair share of nutters who've sent me hate mail. When I was pregnant with Harvey, I had to get a restraining order preventing this one man from coming anywhere near me. He had been bombarding me with letters claiming that we were having a relationship and he kept turning up at my mum's house, where I was staying, and freaking us all out. I've even had hate mail with vile racist abuse about Harvey. And, in the early days of my relationship with Pete, we got letters from a man threatening to knee-cap Pete. The man's letters creepily revealed that he'd been spying on us, and he described what I had been wearing on such and such a date, saying things like *Katie, you looked pretty in that pink dress . . .* It was scary knowing that someone was stalking us like that. We took the threat seriously and called the police. But, however scared I was by these weirdos, I'd always managed to keep a lid on my fear, pushing it to the back of my mind, but at the end of April 2006 something happened that made me feel more vulnerable and more afraid for my family than I ever had before . . .

Pete and I had just returned to the house after a long day of doing an *OK!* shoot in London. It was around ten o'clock at night and, as we were both starving and too knackered to cook, I suggested going out for a curry. We were just about to go when someone buzzed the intercom at our front gate, which was odd, as we weren't expecting anyone.

I checked out the image of a man on the intercom screen, 'Yes,' I said in exasperation, thinking of my dinner.

'Is that Mrs Andre?' asked the stranger.

'Who are you?' I shot back, not in the habit of talking to anyone who'd arrived unannounced at my door and wondering who the hell he was.

'I'm from Sussex Police and I need to talk to you urgently.'

'Right now?' I demanded. 'We were just about to get something to eat.'

'You won't want to eat once you've heard what I've got to say,' he answered.

That sounded ominous, and I was thinking, *Oh no! Now what have I done?*

'But how do I know you're really a detective?' I asked suspiciously. He flashed his badge at the camera and told me his name, not stopping to think further, I let him in. It was only afterwards that I realised how careless I'd been – anyone could make a fake badge.

'Pete,' I called out, 'there's a policeman here and he says we're not going to want dinner when we've heard what he has to say.' Pete immediately came to the door and met the detective and told him he was going to ring the local station to confirm that he was who he said he was. The station did confirm his identity, which was just as well seeing that, by now, he was already in the house, something he was quick to point out – 'You've just let me walk right into your house before you know who I am and you really shouldn't. You've got to step up your security.'

I admitted he was right, then said, 'So what's going on? Why are you here?'

'I can fill you in briefly,' he replied, 'but there's another group of officers coming down from Scotland Yard and they have more details.' *Police officers coming to the house at night? This didn't sound likely to me.*

'Yeah, yeah, this is a wind up isn't it?' I joked back.

He shook his head. 'Not at all. Our intelligence has revealed that there's a kidnap threat against you.'

'No way!' I exclaimed, and even though he looked serious, I was convinced he was bluffing. 'We've been *Punk'd,* haven't we?' It was obviously my turn to have the piss ripped out of me on a hidden camera TV series.

'No,' he insisted, 'This is real.'

I still wasn't sure. It just seemed too surreal to believe. Half an hour later, the other officers arrived at the gate and, after checking their ID, we let them in. Straightaway I said, 'I bet you're the film crew, aren't you?' But they all shook their heads and one of the officers asked if we could sit down as we urgently needed to talk. They were acting their parts well, I thought. I showed them into the lounge, first asking if they could take their shoes off, as I'd just had cream carpets fitted – a wedding present from Richard Desmond, owner of *OK!* magazine, and currently my pride and joy, so absolutely no one – not even high-ranking detectives – was allowed to keep their shoes on in that room! They all sat down looking very serious, but I was more and more convinced that at any minute the prank would be exposed, but Pete was saying, 'This isn't a wind up, Kate.'

'Shut up!' I exclaimed. 'Don't tell me you're in on this as well?' I think all the officers were starting to get seriously pissed off by then that I didn't believe them. I decided to call my manager, Claire.

'So are you on your way over to the house, then?' I said, as soon as she answered.

'What do you mean?' she asked, sounding genuinely surprised.

'Very funny,' I replied. 'I've been *Punk'd*, haven't I?'

'No way!' she exclaimed, and now I started to have a sick feeling in the pit of my stomach that the men really were police officers and that they were in fact telling the truth. I quickly told Claire about the kidnap threat and she said she would drive to the house straightaway with Neville, her partner. I asked the police if we could wait, as I really wanted Claire and Neville to hear what they had to say. As soon as they arrived, I tried one last time to see if they were telling the truth. 'Very funny wind up,' I told them, as I opened the door. And they both stared at me as if I'd gone mad, Claire said, 'I swear, Kate, we would *never* joke about something like this.'

Now I felt anxious. We went and sat in the lounge with the detectives, with me next to Pete, holding his hand tightly for reassurance. 'We can't divulge any names,' one of the Scotland Yard officers said, 'but we've received a tip off from an informant about a plot to kidnap one or both of your children.'

'What!' I exclaimed, panic surging through me. And then we were all bombarding the police with questions. They told us that they believed four people were involved in the kidnap plot, which was planned for when I was out in the car on my own with the boys. The gang would wait until I was on a deserted stretch of road and then force me off it and

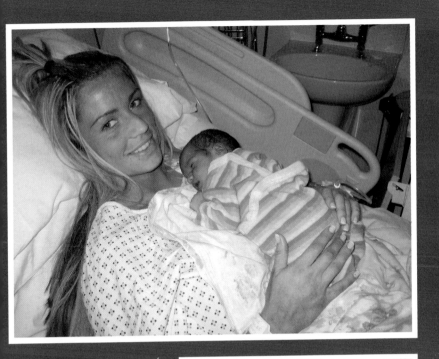

Welcoming Junior into the world.

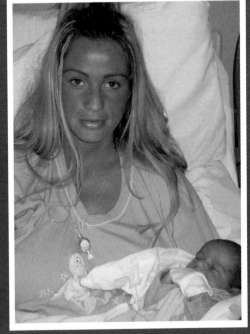

I struggled to bond with
Junior at first as I suffered
from post-natal depression.

A very happy Junior.

Although Harvey took some time to get used to Junior, they are very close now.

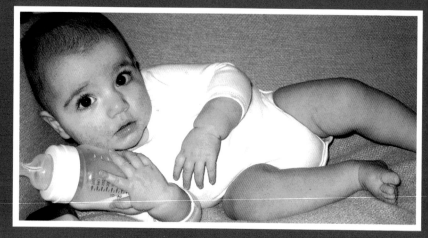

Top: Checking out the props for a photo shoot.

Bottom: Harvey at home.

Junior with his doting
nan...

... and with Yaya.

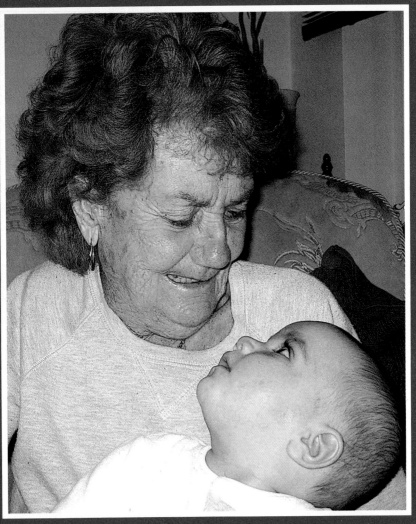
My nan, Essie, with Junior.

A few days before my perfect nan passed away.

Left to right: Me, mum, nan, my aunt Cheryl and my cousin Audrey.

seize either one or both of the boys and then demand a million-pound ransom. They wouldn't try anything while Pete was in the car, of course, because he would be harder to overpower than me. The police revealed that the gang had been watching us and that they knew all our movements and routines. They knew what cars we drove, where we went shopping, where Harvey's school was and even where Junior's nursery was.

Scotland Yard didn't know when the kidnappers were planning to act, but they knew the men had met recently to talk about their plans. From now on, they told us, our lives would have to change dramatically. We would need to have twenty-four-hour police protection. And we wouldn't be able to drive with the boys on our own – we would have to have a police officer accompanying us wherever we went. We would also have to step up security in the house.

I quickly went upstairs and checked on each of the boys as they lay sleeping peacefully. I couldn't believe that anyone could be so evil as to want to kidnap them, two innocent children. It was terrifying to think of my family being under threat. I tried to stay calm and be logical – the police had found out about their plan, so we were safe, and the gang wouldn't be able to get to us now, but I was really shaken by the news. That night, lying next to Pete, I kept imagining driving in the car with Junior and being forced off the road, I imagined masked men taking my son and it was a struggle to put those thoughts out of my head. 'Pete,' I whispered anxiously, holding him tightly, 'Nothing's going to happen to us, is it? The boys are safe, aren't they?'

'Kate, I swear that no one is going to hurt the boys or you.'

And I knew he was right. I couldn't live my life in constant fear, I had to trust that we were safe, otherwise what kind of life would that be?

A few days after the police told us about the plot, I had a promotional trip to China. My first reaction was to cancel it – no way did I want to leave the children at a time like this – but I asked the police what I should do and they said I should go, because I was the target of the plot and, if I wasn't in the country, the gang wouldn't be able to do anything. Also, it would give the police longer to apprehend the gang. Pete also encouraged me to go. I think he could see that, in my present fragile emotional state, it was probably best for me if I was away rather than at home obsessing about the threat. He was supposed to be coming with me to Shanghai, but he decided he had to stay at home. So, very reluctantly, I agreed to go.

*   *   *

I was away for four days. It was the longest time that I'd been away from Pete and the boys and I really missed them all, but work was a great distraction, it took my mind off what had happened. From the moment I got off the plane, I was surrounded by paps taking pictures. They followed me in convoys to the hotel and even managed to get up to the corridor where my suite was. Everytime I opened the door it would be like that scene from *Notting Hill* when Hugh Grant opens his front door to discover they are under siege from the press, with cameras clicking away constantly.

My days were filled with TV and magazine interviews and shoots and everyone was completely fascinated by my boobs! I went to some celebrity event and, as I walked up the red carpet, the people in the crowds were holding up banners with my name on them. I ended up being voted personality of the year, so I can't complain about the attention, as that's what I wanted after all. I texted Pete at least twenty times a day. I knew that the boys were safe, as Pete was with them constantly and we now had twenty-four-hour security in place, but nothing could stop me worrying. Pete was being strong for me, but I know he felt under pressure – plus he was getting hassled by the press, who wanted to know why I was in China without him. They knew we didn't like to be apart for any period of time. Stories started coming out that we were having problems and that our marriage was in crisis. If only they'd known the truth, but we were determined not to tell anyone about the kidnap threat and, even when the *News of the World* did find out somehow, we never commented. The police asked us if we'd like to make a statement to the press, but we said no. We decided it would be better if any official statements came from Scotland Yard. As for our marriage? The kidnappers had wanted to destroy our family, but in fact they'd brought us even closer together.

I felt incredibly vulnerable, though. This kidnap threat had come just at the time when I was trying to get over my Postnatal Depression and had only just found out I was pregnant. For a while, whenever I went out, I felt scared, constantly looking over my shoulder whenever I walked anywhere to make sure I wasn't being followed, checking out the people in the car behind me whenever I drove, wondering *Is it them? Are they the gang?* And it was so stressful knowing that I couldn't just get in my car and go shopping in Brighton, which was usually my little relaxation, because everything had to be planned in advance and I had to have security with me. At the same time, the whole situation seemed surreal – like something out of a film, could this really be happening to me? I've never seen myself as a celebrity, I've always thought of myself as leading a normal life, doing normal things – going to the supermarket, going shopping, taking the kids to school and nursery, going on trips out – without thinking twice about it and now all that had to change.

CHAPTER FIVE

GOODBYE NAN

By the end of May 2006, my lovely nan was still no better. Her lungs were so damaged from years of heavy smoking that they could hardly function and she couldn't breathe properly anymore without the help of an oxygen mask. But she was still all there as a person, and as alert and interested in everything as ever and, whenever I went to see her in hospital, she'd ask after the boys and Pete and we'd talk about what I'd been up to and how she was feeling.

However, she could only speak for a few minutes, after that she'd be gasping for breath and have to put the mask back on. But even as she was desperately struggling to breathe, all she wanted to do was to go home and to walk along the sea front with her dog.

She'd have some good days, when we'd think she seemed well enough to leave because she was so chatty and she was still herself, but then her condition deteriorated. She got an infection and the doctors thought she had pneumonia. She kept pointing over to a particular bed in her ward, saying that patients who were moved onto it always died a few days later. Soon she was moved to that bed herself and she went down hill rapidly after that. Fortunately, she was then taken to intensive care and she seemed to improve. She was put on an even more powerful oxygen mask that covered her face. It pumped in oxygen at such a force that it would have felt like being in a wind tunnel to someone in my nan's state, so while it was good that she could breathe, it was also exhausting for her frail body. The doctors said that, if she came out of hospital, she would have to be on the oxygen mask all the time, but they did seem hopeful that, if she continued as she was, she would be allowed home, which was what she longed for and all of us wanted for her.

At that time, my mum was due to have a major operation and she was in two minds about whether to go ahead with it, because she wanted to be there for her mum. But the doctors reassured her that nan was stable and not likely to get any worse for the moment. So, taking their advice, my mum decided she would have the op. In a bitter twist of fate, on the very same day that my mum had her operation, my nan took a dramatic turn for the worse. But even then she still kept saying, 'I am going to get better, aren't I? I'm going home soon, aren't I?' The awful truth was that she was dying, but none of us wanted to tell her. I so wanted to say, 'Nan, I love you so much, but you're not going home, this is it,' but I just couldn't. And she kept asking the doctor, 'Please tell me I'm going home, I'm getting better, aren't I?' All he would reply was, 'We're doing the best we can.' I felt so powerless to help her, but I really wanted to let her know how much she meant to me, so I sat beside her bed holding her hand, telling her that I loved her, and she'd reply, 'I love you too, Katie.' And as I sat with her, I whispered, 'Nan, I really want to tell you a secret.'

I knew she didn't have long and I wanted to share my news about the baby with her. 'I'm pregnant!' And she looked so pleased, even though she said jokingly, 'Oh God! More kids! Congratulations! How many do you want?'

'I want six!' I told her. And she raised her eyebrows and said, 'God! You two!' I was so glad I had told her.

By early evening, after spending hours at the hospital, I really needed to get back home to see to the boys and to give Harvey his daily injection of medication. I also needed to rest, as I was exhausted. I had terrible morning sickness, I still had Postnatal Depression and we'd just had the terrifying kidnap threat, so it had been a tough couple of weeks spending so much time at the hospital, looking after the boys and trying to work at the same time. 'Please call me if there's any change,' I said to all my relatives and mum's friends at the hospital, and then walked wearily to the car park.

I'd barely been home an hour when Louise, my mum's best friend, called me to say that my aunt Cheryl was trying to get hold of me urgently, as my nan had got much worse. Immediately I was on the phone to Cheryl. 'We need you at the hospital now,' she said, sounding upset, 'They have told us that we've got to make the decision to take her off the oxygen machine.' I just couldn't believe that this was happening now, with my mum still in the recovery room after her major surgery. 'Whatever happens, you make sure that nan stays on that machine and that mum is asked to make the decision. I'm not letting any of you make a decision without her,' I said, stunned and upset at the news. And straightaway I got back into my car and headed back to the hospital, calling Cheryl several times to remind her of her promise not to act without my mum. There we were faced with this appalling situation. We were told that it would be best if we took my nan off her oxygen mask, started giving her morphine and let her go as soon as possible but, meanwhile, my mum had barely come round from her operation, was unable to move and was in no fit state to make a decision.

And even now, throughout all of this, when the doctors had said she could go at any time, my poor nan was still trying to talk to us, struggling to make sense with the mask on, and, when it was taken off, she was gasping and desperately struggling to breathe. It was so cruel, because her mind was completely fine; it was just her body that had packed up. I knew she hadn't got long.

'I know you're trying to do the best for my nan and I know she's going to go, but at least let my mum say goodbye properly,' I exclaimed to the doctor and nurses looking after Nan. I felt so upset.

I knew I had to be the one to break the news to mum. Typically, she put on a brave face, but I knew she wasn't properly with it – she had just had major surgery and she was in agony. 'How's Mum?' she asked. I took a deep breath, 'I'm going to be honest with you Mum. There's never a right time, but this is it now for Nan. She's going to go and the doctors want to move her into another room and take her off the oxygen. But I won't let them do it without you agreeing to it and without you seeing her again.' My poor mum was sobbing and I was crying as well. Mum had been told it would be fine for her to go ahead and have the operation, that Nan's condition wouldn't change and yet now here she was lying in one ward of the hospital unable to move and there was her mum dying in another. Mum had spent so many days and nights at her mum's bedside as she lay in hospital and the one day she wasn't there was the day my nan's condition deteriorated. It was tragic. Reluctantly, Mum agreed that Nan should be allowed to go, but she was desperate to say goodbye to her. 'I have to see my mum,' she kept saying. '*Please.*' But the doctors on her ward were extremely concerned about Mum's own condition – she was still bleeding after the operation when she shouldn't have been and her blood pressure was going down. They said that they couldn't be responsible for what happened to her if she was moved. I did my best to comfort her and then I thought, *I can't stand by and let this happen, Mum has got to see Nan one last time,* and I insisted that Mum was wheeled up to see her.

I returned to my nan's ward, took my family to one side and told them that Mum had agreed that Nan should come off the oxygen. We were all really upset but tried not to show it in front of Nan. All my family, except my mum, were by Nan's bedside, so she was gradually taken off the oxygen and given morphine, and she was getting more and more sleepy, but when you squeezed her hand and said 'Love you, Nan,' she would try to squeeze your hand back and say 'Love you too.' Eventually Mum was wheeled up on her bed and the porters positioned her next to Nan so they were lying side by side. They were actually sharing the same medical equipment, because Mum needed to be monitored. Even though she was in great pain from her operation, she was trying to lean over to hold my nan's hand, saying 'Are you all right, Mum?'

And Nan replied, 'Don't leave me Am, don't leave me,' because she'd overheard the nurses say, 'I'm really sorry, Amy, but you've only got five minutes, because we're not responsible for you in this ward.' That upset me and I asked if I could have a word outside the room and, as soon as the door was shut, I said, 'My mum's mum is dying in there. Please be careful what you say in front of her as she's never going to see her again.'

It was just awful. It was the worst thing my mum could ever have gone through and watching her go through it was just agonising. Back in the room, Mum was trying so hard to be strong and, when Nan asked her again, 'You will come back won't you, Am?' as the porters got ready to wheel her back, she said, 'Course I'll come back, I'll see you in a bit,' and she kissed Nan and gently stroked her hair, knowing that this was the last time she was going to see her, as my nan had just hours to live. My mum would never have had the operation if she'd known her mum was dying, never in a million years . . .

When my granddad Harvey had died, all the family had been there for his last breath and now here was my mum being wheeled away from her mum, crying because she couldn't be there in her mum's final hours. It was heartbreaking. At least my nan was starting to look more peaceful, though, as the morphine took effect. You could talk to her and she'd murmur back, so it seemed as if she could still understand you. A few hours later I went back to my mum's ward and the nurses agreed to let her come and pay one last visit in a wheelchair. She was just allowed five minutes, because she was in agony and physically couldn't sit in the wheelchair any longer than that. I'm so glad that at least she got to see her mum looking peaceful, even if she couldn't be there at the end. By now it was three o'clock in the morning and I was so exhausted I really needed to go home and sleep for a couple of hours before returning to the hospital to be at Nan's bedside – the feeling was that it could still be some hours before Nan passed away.

Back home, I collapsed into bed next to Pete and

then woke up to a text from my aunt saying that Nan had died. I was gutted that I hadn't been there for her last moment. I'd wanted to be there for my nan and for my mum's sake. But as Nan had the rest of the family around her, I hope she felt loved in her final moments. My brother Danny later told me that she opened her eyes and looked towards the window, tried to sit up, then lay back on the pillow and passed away.

I knew Nan was old and she hadn't been well for a long time, but I was still so sad when she died. She was such a great character. I'm very lucky to have had such a lovely nan who adored the boys and really supported me in my career. When we packed up her things in her bungalow, we discovered that she'd kept all my newspaper and magazine cuttings, and I'd never realised that.

The day before her funeral, I had a shoot in Brighton. I was just driving there with Gary, my make-up artist, in the car, when I had a sudden urge to see my nan for the last time. 'Don't think I'm being sick, but I've got to go and see my nan in the funeral home,' I told Gary. I think I wanted to do it for my mum, because I knew she wanted to see Nan but wasn't sure if she was up to it emotionally. So I turned the car round and drove to the funeral home, which was the same place where my granddad had been laid out. It's the smell of those places that always gets me – I guess it's the chemicals they use for embalming, but it's a smell like no other. The funeral director showed me to the room where Nan was laid out and it was so eerie going in there on my own and seeing her coffin in the corner. I really didn't know if I was strong enough to look at her. Mum had chosen a wicker casket for her, saying that, in her life, Nan had been struggling for breath and now she didn't want her to be enclosed in a wooden coffin. Even though the wicker casket didn't look as daunting as a coffin, I still half thought about turning round and leaving without seeing her. But, in the end, I slowly walked up to the casket and looked down at my nan. I was shocked by what I saw – the person lying there didn't look like my nan anymore. She had had curly hair, but it had been straightened and her face looked different because of the way her cheeks had been padded out and because of the way her mouth had been sewn up. I reached out and touched her hand, flinching because it was so cold.

Then I gently kissed her on the top of her head and said, 'See you later, Nan,' as if I was expecting her to answer me. Then I took a few pictures of her with my camera phone, which may sound morbid, but it was something my mum had done when my granddad died. I just wanted to have a final memory of her. Afterwards I called my mum and told her not to go and see Nan, because she really didn't look like herself anymore. But even though it had been upsetting seeing Nan, I was glad that I got to see her one last time. Mum felt that she had to as well, despite what I'd said, and so she got to rearrange Nan's hair to make her look more like she should and dress her in one of her favourite tops and trousers and the flip-flops Nan had always liked to wear.

Unfortunately, my work commitments meant that I didn't really feel I had enough time to grieve for her. On the day of the funeral, I even had to do a shoot for *OK!* for Junior's first birthday. I really wasn't in the best frame of mind for it. I forced myself to smile, but inside I was thinking about my nan and how I was never going to see her again. Straight after that, I had to change into my black dress and dash to the funeral. But the funeral wasn't a sad event – Mum was determined to make it a celebration of Nan's life. So she'd booked the same amazing gospel singers that Pete and me had at our wedding and they sang some of Nan's favourite songs, including 'New York, New York' and 'Moonlight Serenade'. The wicker casket looked beautiful, as Mum had decorated it with flowers such as lupins, irises and roses, so it didn't look formal and forbidding; it looked like something Nan would have liked. And at the end of the service we released six white doves in her memory.

I missed my nan so much. I was so used to seeing her a lot – whenever I went to the hairdresser's in Hove I'd always pop round to her bungalow for a cup of tea and a chat. Over the next couple of weeks, I kept looking at the pictures on my phone that I had of her because I was gutted that I hadn't been there for her last breath and, even though she didn't look like herself, they still comforted me. And I would ring my nan's numbers just to hear her voice on the answerphone – I guess I didn't want to let her go. Then, unfortunately, I broke my phone. I was having a pedicure and dropped my phone into the footspa – and that was it, sadly. I lost all the pictures of my Nan. I was so upset.

She had a brother called Billy, who she was especially close to and he was devastated that she had died before him. He was in a nursing home and was very ill. Two weeks after my nan died, he was in the garden with my mum's cousin when a nurse came and they were both surprised to see that she was holding a dove in her hands. She explained that she'd found the bird on his bed. Apparently Billy reached out and touched the bird and it flew away. He died two weeks later and my mum's cousin told Mum that it must have been Essie, that she had come to get him! It's a nice thought, I suppose, but I think once you're gone, you're gone. But the memory of Nan lives on in my family, because we all still talk about her and we all miss her.

CHAPTER SIX

MY MISCARRIAGE

So there I was dressed as an angel and being driven up London's exclusive Park Lane in a horse-drawn carriage, pulled by six magnificent greys, and the road had been closed especially for me. And, no, this wasn't a dream, it was for real! I was off to Selfridges to launch my first novel, *Angel*, which was published on 5 July 2006. It's the story of a beautiful glamour model who shoots to fame and of her love for two different men — the irresistible, but dangerous

Mickey from a boy-band, who nearly wrecks her career, and the gorgeous, handsome, sexy Cal, a talented premiership footballer who has a problem with commitment . . . I won't give away any more than that!

'How do my wings look?' I asked Nicola, who's part of my management team. 'They're not too big are they?' Then I thought, *What am I on about! The bigger the better!* I'd gone for huge, feathery white wings that were almost as large as me, a short white tunic dress and diamante sandals, so I definitely looked the part. But, as usual whenever I have a launch of anything, I was stressing that no one would turn up and I would be left looking like the saddest, no-mates angel in the world. Fortunately, I needn't have worried. As soon as we drew close to Selfridges, I saw a large pack of photographers waiting for me and hundreds of people pressing against the crash barriers. There was a great turn out for the book signing and *Angel* went straight to number two in the bestsellers. The idea for the launch had been mine – I love coming up with promotional ideas and doing something that no one else has ever done. Its success gave me a huge boost, which was well needed, as I still wasn't feeling myself. Even though I was still taking small doses of anti-depressants and had seen my therapist, I just wasn't the full ticket yet. I kept thinking that I'd got pregnant too soon after having Junior. I didn't feel my body had recovered and I was so worried about getting Postnatal Depression again. Then I'd think, *Oh no, this is good. It's a fresh start. I won't get ill again, I'll show that I can be a good mother.* But the pregnancy had been so stressful, and so many things had happened – the sad death of my nan, the terrifying kidnap threat – and it was all taking its toll on me. I felt incredibly vulnerable and emotional. And I was putting myself under pressure with my work commitments, trying to carry on as usual, even though I had really bad morning sickness and felt absolutely exhausted.

And my state of mind was affecting my marriage yet again. During this time Pete and me ended up having some of our worst arguments, so bad that at one point I really thought that was it, our marriage was over. Things reached crisis point in Cyprus at the end of June, when we were supposed to be doing a shoot for *OK!* Back then it seemed that every time we went there we ended up having massive rows, because Pete claimed that I was always moody in front of his mum and dad, but the fact was it was extremely stressful for me. We had brought both the kids with us and it's always hard taking Harvey to a new environment, as he doesn't like change and it affects his behaviour. And I can't help feeling extra protective of him because he doesn't get the same attention as Junior from Pete's family – I understand why, though, since he's not their grandson, and maybe they're wary of him because of his special needs. I also admit that I can be difficult and, if anyone offers to help me with Harvey, I'll always say 'No, I'm fine, I can cope on my own,' even when I could really do with some help. I know Harvey through and through and he needs careful handling, otherwise he can end up getting upset and having a tantrum. Because of his size and weight, he is very hard to control if he gets in that state and there's always the worry that he'll hurt himself or someone else. If we'd just been visiting Cyprus, things might have been okay, but we were there to work and I was feeling the pressure.

We were staying at the luxurious Four Seasons Hotel in Limassol, as this is where the shoot was going to be, and we were joined by our management team, my sister Sophie and Pete's mum and dad. On our first day, Pete asked if I would mind if Junior slept in his parent's room. I reluctantly agreed, because I know they don't see him as much as they would like to, but it was hard for me and I thought it was a bit odd. Watching his mum picking Junior up and cuddling him took me back to the dark days of my Postnatal Depression and I still had all those negative feelings from my illness. Because Pete's mum was staying with us at that time when it all first started getting to me, somehow seeing her with Junior brought those emotions flooding back. It's so hard to explain and I don't want to upset anyone by saying this – I love the fact that Pete's parents love Junior so much and want to be with him and they look after him so well, as they really are fantastic grandparents. But I still felt like saying, 'Can you give my son back to me now, please?' I realised that I hadn't fully recovered from my depression. I just hoped that one day soon I wouldn't feel like this.

And while I know his mum is fantastic with Junior, she does have a different way of settling him. Whereas I have always put him into his cot and let him fall asleep there, his mum holds him until he goes to sleep. I know she's doing this because she wants to be close to him, but it always means that Junior is harder to settle when he's back with us. And that's exactly what happened on this occasion. When Junior was back with us the following night he wouldn't settle at all because he wanted to be picked up, and I really needed to sleep as I felt so sick from my pregnancy and I also needed to be fresh for the shoot the next day. Whatever I said that evening seemed to irritate Pete and I thought *Fucking Hell! I'm pregnant; I'm not feeling too good. I'm trying to work and look after Harvey, give me a break!'* I felt exhausted, stressed out and on edge. I can't even remember what triggered the row that then followed, but it was probably something really small and it escalated into one of our worst ever arguments, where we said terrible things to each other. 'I don't know what the matter is with you!' Pete shouted at one point, 'I can't fucking handle it anymore!'

'I can't fucking handle it either!' I screamed back, 'I'm carrying your child, where's your fucking respect? If you think you're going to have anything to do with this baby, you can just fuck off and I'll bring it up on my own again. You just go off and take Junior, that's what you want, isn't it?' In the past, like when I'd taken drugs that one time, Pete had threatened to leave and take Junior, and I had never forgotten that threat. It played on my mind and made me feel so insecure. We went to bed without making up. I always hate that.

The next day I felt physically and emotionally shattered. We were trying to do the shoot, smiling away, arms round each other and looking all lovey-dovey for the camera as if there was nothing wrong, but it wasn't working. After our terrible row, I really needed to have Junior in the room with me. Of course I didn't want to split with Pete; of course I didn't want to lose my son. Pete's mum was looking after Junior and every so often would bring him in to see us and then take him away. Looking back, I feel sorry for her, because she was trying to do what was best and I was probably being off-hand with her. But I felt she was hogging Junior and that I had no control over how he was looked after. I felt that Pete and his parents were in their own little group and that they were trying to take Junior away from me. It was too much and suddenly I lost it. 'I'm the mum here, not you!' I shouted at his parents. I didn't care that I was shouting in front of a roomful of people. 'All I want to do is to be a good mum to my son and you just want to fucking take him away from me.' I ran out of the room, unable to take anymore.

Pete followed me upstairs to our hotel suite and continued having a go at me. 'Why is it that every time we come to Cyprus you make things uncomfortable?' he shouted. 'You make no effort with my parents; you make no effort to understand their culture.' I couldn't believe that he was attacking me like this when I was pregnant and felt so stressed. He ended up storming out, leaving me alone. Needing desperately to talk to someone sympathetic, I called my friend Sarah Harding. She was over in the States, as she was seeing the American actor Stephen Dorff and, ironically, she was rowing with him too. After telling her what had been going on, I said, 'I'm going to fly out right now and see you.' I felt so upset that I was seriously prepared to get on a flight there and then to get away from Pete and the situation. My sister, Sophie, helped me pack up all my things and I moved into her bedroom and Sophie made out to everyone that I'd left. I just couldn't face seeing anyone. I called Claire and told her we would have to cancel the shoot, as there was just no way we could pretend that everything was fine when it so clearly wasn't.

It was the very nearest Pete and me have got to breaking up. I don't really know what the cause was, so I can only think that it was my Postnatal Depression because that trip to Cyprus put me under such pressure – we were supposed to be working and yet we had the kids with us, which is stressful, because we were trying to make sure they were kept entertained and doing our work at the same time. Junior was okay, because Pete's mum and dad were looking after him, but I had no one to look after Harvey. To make up with Pete I ended up saying that I would go back and see my therapist and get help, that maybe it was me. I thought, *Just say whatever it takes to make things better*, because I really did want to make a go of my marriage. I love Pete more than anything in the world, so the last thing I wanted to do was break up with him – he was, and is, my life. As you can see, Pete and me are just like everyone else, we have our ups and downs.

* * *

A couple of weeks later we went to the States to shoot my 2007 calendar. This time we didn't take the kids with us – it was just me and Pete and my usual team. We were staying in Las Vegas, at The Palms Hotel, in one of their fantasy suites. Pete and me had the Erotic Suite – an amazingly luxurious suite, all red and black leather, with an eight-foot rotating bed and a mirrored ceiling. It would have been great for someone with a really high sex drive, which, of course, at this point, crippled with morning sickness, I didn't have . . . I got a new tattoo done in Vegas on my right wrist – three hearts: one for Pete, one for Harvey and one for Junior – and I loved that. But the trip wasn't as relaxing as it might have been. For a start, we were being filmed. We hadn't yet signed the new deal for our reality TV show with ITV2, but Claire, our manager, thought we should get footage anyway, so we had a crew filming us the whole time. It was something I didn't need right then, because I didn't feel myself. And even though Pete and me had made up after our bitter argument in Cyprus, I still felt stressed and on edge – everything he did or said at that time annoyed me. Physically, I was freezing cold the whole time, even in the blazing heat. I felt moody, lethargic and had absolutely no energy, I just wanted to sleep. I didn't even enjoy posing for the calendar pictures as I felt so rough. And because no one knew I was pregnant, I was having to pretend to be okay, which is always a stress. 'I'm going to see Dr Gibb when we get home,' I told Pete, feeling anxious. Even though we'd had a scan just before we came away that had been completely normal, I couldn't help worrying that there was something wrong with the baby – it didn't seem right that I was feeling like this.

*   *   *

'Do you think I should be worried about the bleeding?' I said to Pete, just after we'd flown back from the States. For the last three days I had been bleeding, much more than spotting, so much so that I needed to use a pad, which really panicked me. But Pete was quick to reassure me, reminding me that I'd had some bleeding with Junior. All the same, I thought I should get it checked out, especially as we were due to fly to Belize in two days' time for a much-needed holiday, so I phoned Dr Gibb to arrange an appointment to see him that afternoon. We weren't taking the boys on holiday, it was to be just the two of us and a chance for some quality time together, something we badly needed after the rough time we'd been having lately. 'I can't wait for our holiday,' I said to Pete. 'Just to be together, on our own, with no work, no cameras, no filming.'

By now I was four months pregnant. Until now, we'd decided not to find out the sex of the baby and keep it as a surprise, but we thought we'd ask Dr Gibb if he knew what the sex was when he scanned me. I was increasingly worried about the bleeding by then, as it seemed to be getting heavier, but Pete still reassured me. Instead of driving up to London, we decided to go by train, which we never usually do. And we asked Nicola if she wanted to film the journey and the scan for the documentary, thinking that it would make good footage. On the train, Pete and me were excited as we discussed our holiday and I said on camera, 'I've got a secret! I'm four months pregnant and no one knows!' And I lifted up my T-shirt to show off my tiny bump. But then I said, 'Seriously, Pete, what if the scan shows that there's something wrong?'

'I'm sure it will be fine,' he answered.

* * *

'I can't believe you're still not showing, Katie!' Dr Gibb joked as I lay back on the couch getting ready for the scan. At our last scan he'd told me that I was bound to show more with this baby as it was my third pregnancy. Pete said, 'We don't want to know the sex ourselves, but will you see what it is for us?' Dr Gibb agreed as he put the gel on me and the ultrasound device on my belly, and as soon as the images appeared in the screen in front of us, Pete said excitedly, 'So what are we having? Can you see?'

But suddenly Dr Gibb looked serious and was staring intently at the screen. I looked over at Pete and mouthed 'What's the matter?' I had a sick feeling of dread, *Please don't let there be anything wrong with my baby*. And then Dr Gibb turned away from the scan and held my hand and gently said, 'I'm really sorry, Katie, the baby's gone. There's nothing I can do.'

'What!' I exclaimed, totally shocked.

'I'm sorry,' Dr Gibb repeated. 'There's no heart beat, the baby has died.'

'But I can see the baby on the screen,' I said, hardly able to take in his words.

To bring home the reality, Dr Gibb pressed the

ultrasound device against my belly and, whereas before the baby would have instantly reacted, this time it was floppy and it didn't move. My baby was lifeless.

I felt numb with shock. Somehow I managed to ask, 'How long ago do you think the baby died?' And he replied that probably it had been dead for two weeks and that it was extremely fortunate that I had come in now, because, unless the baby was quickly removed, I could get blood poisoning. And then he explained that that's why I had probably felt so cold and moody in America, as I experienced the sudden loss of the pregnancy hormones when the baby died.

By now Pete was in tears, but I was too shocked to cry. I got slowly off the couch and walked into the private waiting room. Pete and me lay in each other's arms on the sofa while Dr Gibb arranged a time for me to have an operation to have the baby removed later that night. I thought about all the other times I had been in this room, looking forward to having my scan, to seeing my baby, and now I was lying there knowing that my baby was dead. I just couldn't believe that this was happening to me now. I'd only just lost my Nan and losing the baby seemed almost too much to bear, *What more can possibly go wrong? Please let nothing else bad happen to us.* Pete was still crying and I was comforting him, saying, 'Don't worry, Pete, these things happen, we'll try for another baby.' As usual, I was putting on a brave face when I should have been coming to terms with the loss myself. I should have been sorting out my own head, but that's just what I'm like.

Dr Gibb arranged that I would go to The Portland Hospital that night to have the operation and, just before we left, I had to take a tablet in preparation. He explained that this would start the process of softening the baby, therefore making it easier to remove in the operation. It was such a horrible thought. I was used to being pregnant now. I'd been carrying the baby for nearly four months and I knew from reading my baby book that it was nearly fully formed. Even though I knew the baby was dead, I almost didn't want to take the tablet because then I really was admitting it was final. For a few minutes I hesitated, as the news hadn't quite sunk in and I thought, *I can't take this tablet. I don't want to harm my baby.* But I knew I had to and so reluctantly I did. Dr Gibb had warned me that I would experience some niggling stomach pains, but after I'd taken the tablet, the pain was actually much stronger than that and I felt sick. When I told Dr Gibb, he said they would have to get me to The Portland as soon as possible, otherwise I was going to be in a great deal of pain.

As we drove through the London traffic to the private hospital, I couldn't believe how the day had turned out. All we had wanted to do was to check the baby was okay and let Dr Gibb find out the sex and now this had happened. It's a shock to anyone to have a miscarriage, even if you're only a few weeks pregnant, but the pain is almost indescribable when the baby has been growing inside you for four months and you've watched its development on the scans, seen it move around . . .

By the time we arrived at The Portland, the pain had intensified and I was feeling very sick. It was so horrible coming here of all places. This was where I'd given birth to Junior; this is where I had been planning to have this baby. 'I just can't believe this is happening,' I said to Pete, 'I should be going in here to have a baby, not losing one.' We were shown to our room and it was exactly the same as the room I stayed in after I'd given birth to Junior, which made me feel even worse. As I lay down on the bed, so many conflicting thoughts were going through my head. I couldn't believe that I was about to have an operation, that I was losing my baby, and part of me thought, *I don't want this operation, I want to keep my baby, I want to have a baby*. I wanted to turn the clock back to two weeks ago when my baby was still alive. All too soon it seemed it was time for me to go down to theatre. Pete was by my side and he was still so upset, but he did his best to comfort me. I still hadn't even cried.

In theatre, because of my extreme needle phobia, I begged the anaesthetist to put me under without using a needle; I just didn't think I could cope with that as well. I lay there and looked up at the clock. It was seven twenty-five. Just over a year ago I'd been lying on an operating table in The Portland about to have the caesarean to deliver Junior, staring at the clock and thinking, *In half an hour, I'm going to have a baby* and I'd been so excited. But this time in half an hour I wouldn't have a baby. And then the anaesthetist put the mask over my face and I started losing consciousness and that was the only good thing about that day, as weirdly I love having general anaesthetics. I remember Pete holding my hand and I was looking at him as I slipped into unconsciousness. It can't have been nice for him watching me in that state, but he was there for me, supporting me all the way.

When the nurses woke me up in the recovery room and told me that it was all over and I was fine, I still felt physically cold and emotionally shattered. After an hour, I was wheeled upstairs to my room. Feeling totally numb, Pete and me watched *Big Brother* – another flashback to the year earlier when I'd just had Junior and we'd watched the programme together. But last time I'd lain in a room like this I had a beautiful baby boy in my arms, a new life to celebrate, now here I was and I had nothing.

I was desperate to know why I'd had a miscarriage. Dr Gibb explained that there are many causes and it is much more common than I had realised – one in four women who become pregnant will have a miscarriage. The most common cause is a genetic abnormality in the baby. But Dr Gibb explained that he couldn't tell me why I'd had a miscarriage without tests being carried out on the baby. I was convinced that it would help me come to terms with our loss if

I knew what had gone wrong, so I asked if they could carry out the tests. I also wanted to know whether the baby had been a boy or a girl. Pete didn't want to know any of this, but I needed to. Some people might question this and think why didn't I just accept that what had happened was nature's way, but I needed answers. If a chapter's open on something in my life, I like to know that I can close it and move on and I needed to close the chapter on this experience.

I was deeply upset by the miscarriage and I felt like a failure. I thought, *Fucking hell, why is this happening to me?* I couldn't help wondering if it had been triggered by that terrible row Pete and me had in Cyprus and because I'd been so stressed. All the pregnancy books tell you that stress is bad for you and the baby. I'd also still been suffering from Postnatal Depression and I wondered if that had affected the baby. So I knew, if I didn't find out what had been wrong with the baby, I would obsess about it and blame myself.

I had to pay for the tests and it took six weeks to get the results. I discovered the baby was a girl. *I wonder if I will ever have another girl?* I thought to myself, and I couldn't help feeling sad. She had something called Turner's Syndrome, where the baby is missing all or part of one of their sex chromosomes. It occurs in approximately one in two thousand births and in as many as 10 per cent of all miscarriages. Pete and me checked on the Internet for more information and were able to see what the baby would have been like if she had survived. She would have been smaller than average and she would have needed growth hormones; she would have had ovarian failure and would have needed oestrogen from puberty; she would have been infertile; and she may have had a heart abnormality and mild hearing loss. Finding this out really helped me accept what had happened. I understood there was a reason for the miscarriage – my Postnatal Depression and the row in Cyprus had not caused it.

Pete took the miscarriage quite hard and I did too at first, but as soon as I got the test results, I felt that I could try and move on. What didn't help was that just three days after my miscarriage the press got hold of the story and that really hurt us. I thought they could have at least given us time to recover from this before splashing it in the papers. The miscarriage had been such a deeply personal and upsetting experience and we were struggling to come to terms with it, we really didn't need the attention.

Shortly after that we went on our holiday. We had been so looking forward to it and we were desperate to get away. We love our work and we love working together, but we often don't get quality time together. All too often our lives are filled with the same routine: come home late from work, sort out the kids, eat, have a bath, go to bed, wake up and work again. And I think the stress of not unwinding had built up with us. We were going to be away for two weeks on a beautiful remote island in Belize, Central America. We were told it was like the Maldives, a place we love and where we spent our honeymoon. There were only seven luxury beach villas on the island and it sounded perfect. We would be able to completely relax, swim, sunbathe and have treatments, or so we hoped. The reality was very different. The first thing that put us off was when we were told we couldn't go in the water because there were sea urchins that would sting us – great! Who wants to go to an island and be told they can't swim?! Pete and me were also the only people staying on the island, which would have been fine if the staff were friendly, but as it was, they were miserable-looking sods who didn't seem to want to do anything for us, which made us feel so uncomfortable. Worse, there were spiders everywhere, and I mean everywhere! At night we had to sleep under a mosquito net and, in the morning when we woke up, the outside of the net would be covered in spiders. So everytime we went to bed we'd be worrying about spiders and wondering if any had managed to get into the bed, which meant we couldn't sleep. Every five minutes one of us would be going, 'Ugh! What was that!' And yet again Pete had a disaster with a sea creature – in the Maldives he'd nearly lost a finger when he was fishing and he caught a giant ray. On what turned out to be our only good day, some guys took us out on a boat so we could go scuba diving and swim with sharks and fish. Before we dived in, they gave us some words of advice: 'Whatever you do, when you're near the fish, keep your fists clenched and don't wave your fingers at them.' So what does Pete do? He ignores the advice, waves his fingers at the fish and a shark bit him . . . typical! Luckily he was fine. Not long after that the naturalist Steve Irwin got killed by a sting ray, which made me think I was never going to go scuba diving again, as we'd been swimming with rays that day and I'd had no idea they could be so deadly.

We were supposed to be staying in Belize for two weeks, but we only lasted three days. All in all, the holiday was a disaster, though it did give me time to reflect on what had been happening in my life recently.

CHAPTER SEVEN

HARVEY'S PROGRESS

'Love you, Harvey,' I said, sitting on his bed and kissing him good night.

'Love you, Mummy,' Harvey replied, smiling.

'Do you want a cuddle?' I asked him, and he nodded, replying, 'Sss', because he can't say yes, and reached up his arms. As I held him tight, I was filled with such happiness that Harvey was now showing affection. It had taken until he was nearly four years old before he started to say 'love you' and want hugs.

Before that you could ask him for hug and he would give you one, but now he asks for a hug because *he* wants one and he's become a really affectionate little boy. He definitely knows his own mind, because sometimes I'll say 'Does Harvey want a . . .?' and I'll leave him to fill in the answer and he'll reply 'Cuddle' and then say 'No!' – he lets us know exactly what he wants. It's such a wonderful change, because there was a time when I thought he would never be able to express his emotions; that he would stay in his own little world. And even though he still has lots of medical and behavioural problems because of his condition, he's come on so much over the last couple of years.

Harvey was born with a rare disorder called Septo-Optic Dysplasia (SOD), which means that he's visually impaired and he's deficient in all the hormones the body needs to function healthily. He may also have developmental problems with the front part of his brain and he has cortisol deficiency, which affects his stress responses and makes it harder for him to fight off illness and infection and cope with shock. He has to have medication three times a day every day, including an injection of growth hormones, to make his hormone levels normal. His cortisol deficiency is extremely serious, because if he gets ill or has an accident, he needs an extra cortisol injection straightaway to help his body cope, as he can't produce enough cortisol himself; without it he could potentially have a fit and die. We also think he may have suffered some kind of brain damage before his condition was fully diagnosed, because his development has been slow.

From the moment he was diagnosed – first with his visual impairment at six weeks old and then with SOD when he was a year old – Harvey has been in and out of hospital to have his conditions monitored and to check that his medication levels are right. There have also been those really terrifying times when he's been rushed to hospital for an emergency – several times when his temperature has rocketed alarmingly and, of course, after his accident on New Year's Eve 2007. Poor Harvey, he's only five years old and he's been through so much and, no matter what he's had to deal with, he's always been such a brave little boy. Just before my wedding in September 2005, he spent six weeks in Great Ormond Street Hospital being tested, because the doctors were so concerned about his weight gain. I missed him so much and hated not having him at home with me. At that time he was only three and a half, he barely ate anything and yet he weighed five and a half stone – the weight of an eleven-year-old. It was extremely dangerous for him to weigh so much, as it put such a strain on his lungs and his heart. He could have had a heart attack. The doctors discovered that his weight was a result of his condition. We have to monitor him carefully now and check what he's eating and make sure he gets enough exercise. By the age of five he weighed seven stone, but he wasn't gaining any more weight and he had grown taller and become more mobile.

It took Harvey a lot longer to learn to walk because he is visually impaired, but now he can walk and run confidently. He loves going on the trampoline in the garden and loves playing rough and tumble games like any other little boy. However, he doesn't like walking in places he's not familiar with, because he can't see his surroundings and it frightens him. Take him out of his environment, to a shopping centre, for example, and there's no chance that he'll want to walk. He'll panic and ask for his 'black chair', which is what he calls his wheelchair. To him his 'black chair' is his comfort zone and it's where he feels safe. And even though I know he can walk, I'd rather he sat in his chair and was happy. Otherwise he only needs to hear a noise he doesn't like and he'll throw himself back on the floor, have a tantrum and there I am in the middle of a shopping centre unable to lift him. Still, I want to be able to take Harvey out and about with me – I don't want him to miss out. Gradually it has got easier to take Harvey out and he now loves going on the beach, playing with pebbles and throwing them in the water. He will ask to go shopping with me too, which shows he must enjoy it. Whenever we're in the shops together, he'll ask me for a black clothes hanger, then he'll sit happily in his wheelchair flicking it.

But it took me a while before I was ready to accept that Harvey needed a wheelchair and I was really negative about the idea. I've always tried to keep Harvey's life as normal as possible and I didn't want people to look at him differently. When he got too big to push around in a buggy for toddlers, I bought a Maclaren buggy that was designed for bigger children who are disabled. When I took Harvey out in that, I found it so much easier to push him. It was a turning point, because I thought *Actually, I don't care what anyone else thinks, he needs this special buggy and that's all that matters.* But it still left me with the problem of what to do if I wanted to take Harvey and Junior out on my own, because I couldn't push two buggies. So I asked Maclaren to make a double buggy that was suitable for Harvey. But the trouble was Harvey didn't like Junior at the time and, if Junior made any noise, Harvey would whack him, so we had to stop using that buggy, which meant that I couldn't take the boys out together on my own. After a few months, Harvey outgrew his new buggy, and it was a nightmare trying to get him in and out of it, as it really put a strain on my back. Eventually my mum suggested we try out a wheelchair for him. I had my doubts, but as soon as I saw Harvey in it, I realised he had to have one, because it was so much more comfortable for him and so I arranged for him to have his own wheelchair made to fit him. Maybe one day he won't need it when we go out, and he will be more confident about walking around places he doesn't know, but for now he does.

In September 2006, Harvey started school full time. He goes to a special school for visually impaired

Harvey's first day at school.

Bottom right: Trying out a new hairstyle with one of my hairpieces.

Pete and I getting ready for my step-dad's 40th birthday party.

Bottom: Mum, Sam, Sophie, Paul, me and Pete at the restaurant.

Top: Sophie and Sam
Bottom: Daniel
and Louise.

Top: My mum, Amy.

Middle: Sophie and my stepdad, Paul.

Bottom: Me and Pete with Sophie and Sam

Girls just wanna have fun. My mum's mates: Mary, Louise, Eve, mum and Linda.

Me and Pete heading out for the night in Dubai.

Enjoying the cocktails!

My gorgeous husband Pete.

children – he had already been to nursery there and loved it. The staff are brilliant and I am so glad he has a place, because he has made so much progress. But it wasn't easy – we had to fight the council to get them to pay for Harvey's fees and had to go to appeal. I now have such sympathy for other parents of children with special needs. I knew that this school was the right place for Harvey – mainstream school was not an option, as there was no way he could cope. He's doing really well there, so much better than I ever expected. He's learning to read and he knows all the letters of the alphabet. If you ask him to point out the letters for his name, he can. He can count up to thirty and he knows all his colours and shapes. In fact, he knows more shapes than me! He's forever pointing out hexagons and pentagons and I wouldn't have a clue that's what they were without him telling me. He can also use touch-screen computers – he has two in his bedroom – and he absolutely loves playing games on them. His ability to use the computer never ceases to amaze me; he's way better at using a computer than I am! I can just about manage to switch one on, but that's it. I'm seriously thinking of doing some kind of computer course, because I feel I'm being left behind. I'm not very good with technical things. I've got a blackberry phone, yet I've got absolutely no idea how to use email or any of the other different functions and I just use it for phoning and texting. My friends take the piss out of me and say I may as well just have an old brick of a handset.

While Harvey has made such good progress, life with him is a challenge and I think it always will be. I love him so much, he's completely unique. I wouldn't want him to be any different. But having a child with his special needs can make family life tough at times. For instance, he is incredibly sensitive to certain noises. We had thought that he had something wrong with his hearing. When he heard a sound he wasn't familiar with or wasn't expecting to hear, he would frequently react by having a violent tantrum. But the hearing specialist discovered that his hearing was perfectly normal, it's just that, if he hears something he isn't expecting he gets upset because he can't see what's making the noise. It was good to know that there was nothing wrong with his ears, but the fact remains that he is incredibly sensitive to sound. He has a thing about the sound of doors closing and the sound of baby gates being clicked. At home, even if he is upstairs in his room and hears a door being closed downstairs, he goes mad. If you warn him you're about to shut the door, he'll be fine, but if he hears it and he isn't expecting it, he gets very upset. Whenever I take him to Great Ormond Street for one of his many check-ups and assessments, they provide a special room for Harvey where he can be on his own with me, as he cannot bear the sounds of doors banging around him in the waiting room. Recently we had an appointment with a specialist at the hospital and we were halfway through the assessment when Harvey heard a door close from somewhere far along the corridor. He went nuts, throwing himself back and crying. The specialist asked what the matter was and I told him that Harvey was reacting to the sound of the door. I think the specialist was surprised, because he said, 'But that was a long way away!'

'He absolutely hates the sound of it,' I replied. 'First of all, he hated the sound of cutlery against the tables in restaurants, so it was a nightmare ever going out to eat with him. Now he's okay with that and it's the sound of doors shutting that upsets him.' I asked if he thought it was something Harvey would grow out of. The specialist replied that it seemed as if Harvey had built up an aversion to the sounds of doors that was similar to people hating the sound of chalk on a blackboard and that he may or may not grow out of it. In the meantime, we have to be so careful in the house and practically tiptoe around. Sometimes when we have guests over and have managed to persuade Harvey to come down out of his room – which always takes some doing because, given the choice, he will always prefer to be in his room – he will be perfectly happy playing with his toys till one of the guests, not realising Harvey's problem with noise, shuts a door and ruins Harvey's good mood. He'll have a tantrum, cry and say, 'I want to go to bed!' Which means he wants to go back to his bedroom where he feels safe. The doctors have told us that children with his condition aren't usually very sociable and I can see this with Harvey, he doesn't like being around people he doesn't know and he doesn't like fuss from them. So while I wish he could be with us downstairs seeing other people and being part of the family, I've had to accept that's not what Harvey always wants and I don't want to force him. He likes his own company. Sometimes he'll play on his keyboard and I will play a few notes and he'll take my hand and move it away and say, 'No, Mummy!' He would rather play on his own. He also has very strong views about what music he likes. Whenever we're driving anywhere he has to listen to R&B and it has to be on loud and he doesn't like anyone talking over it. Fortunately, Pete and me both like R&B. I just hope for their sakes that Junior and Princess do as well!

Harvey is also on the autistic spectrum. Like other children on the spectrum, he's obsessed with routine. He also flicks objects repeatedly close to his face, and can often seem to be in his own little world when he's engrossed with playing with his toys – however many times you try and get his attention, he will completely ignore you. He is getting more sociable, though, and he does recognise people. His communication skills have also improved. Now he wants to join in conversations and tell us things. He's forever pointing things out that he can see. He'll say, 'Rectangle book!' and he will want me to reply 'Yes, Harvey, rectangle book, well done!' If I don't answer straightaway and give him praise as a reward, he'll get upset. He's also starting to be able to say what he wants, though he does get frustrated sometimes and lashes out when we don't immediately understand him. When you're with him, he wants your full attention, which can be hard on the other children. Hopefully, when his communication skills improve even more, his behaviour will too, because he'll be able to express himself and be understood.

Whatever you say to Harvey he remembers it exactly and then repeats it later, and in the right context. A funny and embarrassing example of this was shown on our TV reality show. Pete had been taking acting classes and was asking everyone 'Are you patronising me?' to test out his dramatic skills. Well, when he asked Harvey, he didn't quite get the answer he was expecting, 'Fuck off!' Harvey told him. I know I swear a lot, but I don't agree with children swearing and I make a real effort not to swear in front of the kids, so I can only think that maybe my sister Sophie had said it in front of him. She's only young and probably thought it was funny. Straightaway Pete told him 'No, that's a bad word!' But, even though he was right, I was more laid back about it, thinking that, if we ignored it, Harvey wouldn't want to say it again. In fact, come to think of it, the only times Harvey ever repeats the word is when he sees my sister, so he must have learnt it from her.

Just as Harvey has been learning about the world around him, we've been learning how best to communicate with him. We've discovered that we have to explain to Harvey exactly what we are going to do all the time so he is prepared and that this is all to do with his visual impairment. For example, I can see a jogger, say, in the distance who is running in my direction and my eyes have prepared my brain for that fact, but Harvey can't see that person in the distance. As far as he's concerned, one minute there's no one there and the next minute someone's right in front of him and he might well lash out because he's so surprised. So we have to warn him about what to expect. At bedtime we have to say, 'Night, Harvey, lights off, door closed, gate click.' In the morning, I have to explain that I'm going to get him dressed, that we're going to have breakfast, put his shoes on and then, to make it a game, I'll add, 'Then we're going to get into Mummy's . . .?' And he'll say 'Black car!' We have to keep going over the routine with him and that seems to make him much happier. Of course, one consequence of that is that we can never rush him. At times that can be frustrating, because I know I'm going to be late for a job, but then I think, *This is our life, and this is what Harvey is like. If I'm late, it's tough, my son comes first.*

I've noticed he doesn't have quite as many tantrums as he did when he was younger, probably because he is getting better at expressing himself. But he still has them and he's very difficult to cope with when he loses it. He can throw himself back violently and then find the nearest object and chuck it. He has managed to smash his bedroom window with a toy because he was frustrated that the Tweenies were on his TV when he wanted to watch Barney, for example. And he has broken three televisions in the past by picking them up and smashing them on the ground, so I've had to have his touch-screen computer and flat-screen TV attached to the wall. This behaviour can cause tension at home, as Pete keeps saying that Harvey should only have soft toys, because one day he could really hurt one of the other kids by throwing something, but I argue that there aren't any soft toys that are educational for him. Pete also thinks that he shouldn't have any toys in his room if he's going to throw them, but I say that it wouldn't be fair on him. Anyway, most of the time he's perfectly happy in his room and hopefully the throwing is just a phase. We do discipline him so he understands such behaviour is wrong, though. I use the naughty step technique. Harvey understands that if he throws something he has to pick it up, say sorry and go and sit on the naughty step and count to thirty. So, although he's being told off, he's also practising his counting – and if he gets it wrong I make him start again! Because he loves routine so much, he's turned this into a game and will often throw something, then proceed to tell himself off using our exact words and go and sit himself down on the naughty step.

He loves having other children around him, but you have to watch him all the time. I would never leave him alone with the baby or with Junior, even though the boys get on much better now and will sometimes play together. He will often ask for his brother, but Junior is wary of him because he's been hit in the past. Junior also doesn't get that close to Harvey unless he knows he's in a good mood. He knows that Harvey is different from the other children he plays with at nursery, though that doesn't stop him from being cheeky and he'll sometimes nick a toy Harvey is playing with and run off with it, knowing that Harvey will go ballistic. But it doesn't last long, as I tell Junior to give the toy back and say sorry, then Harvey will say, 'Thank you, Junior.' At bedtime they will sometimes have a bath together, as I really want the two of them to get on. But this is another thing Pete and me slightly disagree on. Pete says that Harvey is on so much medication that, if he wees in the bath, Junior might be exposed to it, but I don't think it's a problem. Harvey has been much better with Princess than he was with Junior. It doesn't annoy him when she cries, and he's always blowing her kisses. By the age of five, Harvey still wasn't toilet trained and so, when Princess was born, I felt as if I had three babies, because I had three of them in nappies, which is hard work, I can tell you . . .

Probably the thing that holds Harvey back the most is his visual impairment, because it affects his behaviour. But we think he can see a lot more than we realise. Before Harvey was talking, it was difficult to work out what he could or couldn't see, but now he can communicate better, we are finding out more about what he can see. He recognises family and friends when they come into a room and he says hello to them. When we're in the car together and I ask him to tell me the colour of the lorry next to us, he's able to. At Pete's house in Cyprus, Harvey loves standing at his bedroom window, pointing down at the pool and saying, 'Blue rectangle swimming pool.' It's so much more than I ever thought he would be able to see when his condition was first diagnosed.

But I do worry sometimes that our other children miss out on our attention and that they don't get to go places. This is where I wish I had more support from Dwight. As any one who has a disabled child knows, it is important for the family to have a break from caring for them sometimes, and I would love it if Dwight could have Harvey for the occasional weekend. This isn't because I want to get rid of Harvey, but because I sometimes feel Junior suffers when so much of our attention is on his brother. I'd like to be able to take Junior to places like the theme park at Chessington. I don't want to leave Harvey at home, but if I take him as well, inevitably the trip becomes all about calming him down and making sure he is all right and so our attention is off Junior. However, there's no way I will allow Harvey to spend a weekend with Dwight until he sees him more regularly, until he can confidently give him his medication and until I know that Harvey is comfortable with him and would feel safe at his house. Harvey just doesn't know Dwight well enough yet and, because of his special needs, it would confuse and upset him too much to be away from us.

Dwight does see Harvey every now and then, but, as I said, I don't think it is often enough. During term time he will go and see him at school, but it's never for very long. My mum plays a strong part in caring for Harvey and is the one who arranges these visits. She told me that Harvey calls Dwight 'Dad' but he also calls Pete 'Dad'. To me, Pete is Harvey's dad, because he is the one bringing him up. Dwight rings my mum every week to check on Harvey, but I would be fine if he rang me, as there's no bitterness between us. Pete and me have also said that he is welcome to come and see Harvey at the house to get to know him better and so I can see that Harvey is comfortable with him, but he hasn't taken me up on the offer.

Harvey is such a character and, on the whole, he is such a happy little boy. I used to worry about all the things he might not be able to do because of his visual impairment. I worried that he would miss out on so much, but he has such a full, active and happy life. He goes to school like other children; he plays like other children do; and he loves swimming, horse-riding, music, and playing on his keyboard and computer. I recently watched a documentary about visually impaired young adults who were living together in sheltered accommodation where they were supervised; part of me would like to think that Harvey might be able to live like that one day as well. But I imagine that he will always live with Pete and me, and we are both happy for him to do that. The truth is I would worry about him so much if he lived away from home. I want him to be safe with me; I want that for all my children.

CHAPTER EIGHT

ANNIVERSARY

1 September 2006, our first wedding anniversary. We'd had quite a year . . . And, in spite of all the difficulties we'd had to deal with – my Postnatal Depression, the kidnap threat and the miscarriage – we had stuck together and got through it. You'd expect to have problems later on in a marriage, but we seemed to have had them all in our first year! We celebrated in style on a luxury yacht in Antibes, in the South of France, and I think we felt especially

close to each other, after everything we'd been through.

As everyone knows, we love our bling and buying each other presents, so, for our anniversary, I bought Pete a ring covered with diamonds, all the way round the band, and he completely spoiled me – he bought me a massive pink heart-shaped diamond ring. Some weeks earlier I had told the guy who makes our jewellery that I wanted a ring with a big pink diamond heart and was all set to buy one for myself, but Pete beat me to it. I have to admit that I've now got so many diamonds I actually don't want anymore . . . I'm blinged out!

Since Pete and me have been together, there have been plenty of stories claiming that our marriage is in crisis and they're all bollocks! Yes, we bicker, but all couples I know bicker, and it's not because we're about to split up. The only real time we came close to it was when my Postnatal Depression put such a strain on our marriage. We are feisty with each other, but we're completely equal, we give as good as we get. Our relationship is definitely stronger than when we first met and it's more solid and more complete because of the children. Now it's as if we're one as a couple and we do everything together. If Pete isn't in the house, it feels weird to me and, if I'm not there, he feels the same.

Our relationship has still got the intensity and passion that it had from the start. I still look at him and think he's absolutely gorgeous. He's so good looking and so it's not hard keeping that sexual attraction alive. We went through that phase when I went off sex because I was depressed and I was on medication and now we look back and laugh about it, though it was a problem at the time. But we got through it and I say to anyone I know, 'If we've got through that then so can you.' Pete is always obsessing over his looks, especially his weight. He worried when I was pregnant with Junior that he had really piled on the pounds, but I never noticed. To me he always looks like he's got a good body – that's never been an issue. I just think he's fit. Obviously he doesn't have the ripped abs he had in his 'Mysterious Girl' days, but he said he was really skinny then and I prefer a man to be a man. I absolutely love his body; it's only him who has a problem with it. I love the pretty boy look that he's got. I'm always teasing him that he looks gay. I mean it as a compliment to gay men and to Pete, because all the gay men I know really take care of themselves and look really good. I don't know any other straight men who get their nails done, but I think it's nice when men look after themselves.

But it's not just about his looks. In Pete I really have found my soul mate and I love him so much. I love the way he's so good with the kids; I love the way he handles me, looks out for me and looks after me; and I love how he's great in bed. He's talented, he's ambitious, he works hard, he's not lazy and he doesn't ponce off me. I'm not bored at all and I definitely haven't got the itch to go looking anywhere else. Our relationship is different from all the others I've had because we've never played games with each other. In the past, when I've first got together with someone, I admit that I have played games – I tried to make them jealous and wanted to know that I had their full attention. But Pete and me have never been like that – we were totally honest about our feelings from the beginning. I know that if Pete's out, girls are bound to come up to him, not only because he's famous but because he's such a good-looking guy too and he's got the charm and personality to go with it.

But I don't feel threatened one little bit. Though, of course, we went through a stage where we were both obsessed about each other's exes and it really mattered to us who we had each slept with. I did feel threatened because Pete had slept with so many women and, even now, if a girl claims to have kissed him and I ask him if he can remember her, he won't be able to. And if I then say, 'Would you remember if you had fucked a girl in the past or not?' His reply will be no. He's had that many women, he's lost count. But I'm not bothered anymore. His past is his past and I've had my past too, but when you marry someone, you marry them to be with them for life. We've gone through so much together and he hasn't experienced that with any other girl, so our relationship is unique. Having said that, I wouldn't say that I trust him 100 per cent; I would never trust a man 100 per cent. But I know for a fact that he wouldn't want to risk losing everything he had by being unfaithful for one night.

We've both got quite similar characters – the way we think, the way we're both into our families, the way we're both so ambitious, the way we're sexually compatible, even in the way we've both had panic attacks in the past. But we're very different as well. I'm always the one who will cut to the chase in any situation. When we're interviewed, Pete will take so long to get to the point of what he wants to say, whereas I'll just come out with it! But that's just Pete and I wouldn't want to change him.

I can't fault Pete as a father. I've said it before and I'll say it again, any man can fill a pram, but it takes a real man to be a dad and Pete is a fantastic dad. I never would have been with him in the first place unless he accepted Harvey and he did more than that – he treats him as his own son. Looking back, I realise that Harvey was tiny when Pete and me met – only a year and a half old – so Pete's been with him and seen him progress. To me Pete is Harvey's dad. Pete is brilliant with both Junior and Harvey. I never think that he must love Junior more, but obviously he's going to have a different bond with Junior because he's his blood child, and yet he treats them both equally. It's exactly how my stepdad Paul brought up me, my brother Daniel and Sophie. Sophie is his biological daughter, but there's never been any difference in how Paul treated the three of us.

* * *

As well as my anniversary, I had two really fun things to do in September. One was interviewing the actor Rupert Everett and the other was being dressed by the designer John Galliano. Rupert and me were photographed in a James Bond-style shoot. I got to pout and wear some gorgeous evening dresses, and Rupert wore black tie and looked mean and moody – it was such a laugh! It was great to meet him, as he stars in one of my favourite films, *My Best Friend's Wedding*. It was the first time I had ever had to interview anybody who was a somebody and I was shitting myself with nerves! But then I thought, *It's a challenge, just do it!* And, actually, I loved it, because I got to ask him questions that other people probably wouldn't ask him – quite cheeky ones, of course – and it was good practice for my chat show.

I was invited to Paris Fashion Week by John Galliano to see his show. I love his clothes, so I was really thrilled when he said that he wanted to dress me for it and sent over a few dresses for me to try on. People always seem to think that, because of my boobs, clothes won't fit me, that they'll be too tight, but in fact half of the dresses were too big! I ended up choosing a figure-hugging, slinky black dress that I loved, and which I felt really good in. And he gave me the most gorgeous pair of Dior shoes, black with really high, thin silver heels. When I flew over to Paris for the show itself, John's boyfriend came to my hotel to get me dressed and I had my hair and make-up done by the people John Galliano uses – I loved the look they gave me. I met John before the show and he was a really nice guy. I also went backstage and saw all the models and it was fascinating watching them get ready. Wherever I went I had photographers taking pictures of me, and I thought, *Oh! I'm in France and I'm recognised here too!*

I had front-row tickets for the show and, as I sat there with Nicola from my management, we were both giggling, saying, 'Look at little us sitting here,' because we were on the same row as such famous people, including Janet Jackson. Then Demi Moore and Ashton Kutcher arrived and sat on the same row too. It was such a performance when they walked in with their bodyguards and they got so much press attention. I thought, *Holy shit, it's only a fashion show!* I loved the show itself, though I was surprised it was so short – it only seemed to last about eight minutes – but maybe that's normal for the world of fashion. One day, I would love to do a catwalk show – either for someone else's clothes or for my own, so we'll have to see . . . John and his boyfriend asked me to join him and his friends for dinner that night, but I had a shoot to do early the next morning, so I couldn't. Instead Nicola and me sat on my bed in my hotel suite and played cards. Who says I don't know how to enjoy the high life!

CHAPTER NINE

A DREAM COME TRUE?

As you've heard me say before, I've always wanted to be a singer. As a teenager, it hadn't been my ambition to be a glamour model – I wanted to be a pop star. But for some reason my singing career had never got off the ground. I'd been promised so many record deals, but none of them had ever materialised. And then I took part in the Eurovision show to find the UK's singer for 2005 and what a total disaster that was. It was well over a year before I could actually bear to watch my performance and, when I did, I thought I was absolutely diabolical. I'm embarrassed by everything about it. I was singing a song that I hated because it was pitched too high for my voice, and the pink rubber catsuit which I thought would disguise the fact that I was five months pregnant actually made me look bigger than I was. Eurovision is the only thing that I've done that I've ever regretted and it was the worst thing I could have done for my singing career. I couldn't help thinking that it had damaged my credibility, and I wasn't sure that anyone would take me seriously as a singer ever again.

For a while after Eurovision my confidence was too battered to even think about getting back into the studio. But singing 'A Whole New World' with Pete on *Children in Need* in November 2005 helped turn things round for me, because I was singing a ballad which I loved and which suited my voice and I felt my performance proved that I could sing. We also received such a positive response afterwards from people who wanted us to release it as a single. That got Pete and me thinking about our music careers. We decided that we wanted to release an album of duets together. We wanted to sing love songs that described what it felt like to be in love, I definitely didn't want to sing songs about breaking up. But, if we ever do split up, we can always release an album of duets about being broken hearted! So we met up with Nicky Graham and Deni Lew, who had both worked with me on my Eurovision song. While I hadn't liked the song, I had got on really well with them and loved their way of working, so I took up singing lessons again and Pete and me began work on the album.

Then we came up with the idea of doing the album for charity. It would be great to be able to give something back to the public and, because of Harvey's condition, there are several charities that are particularly close to my heart. There were record companies that wanted to sign us up, but when it came down to it they didn't seem to have enough faith in us. They offered us shit deals and expected to control everything. 'Stuff that,' Pete and I said to each other. We weren't wannabes – we both had successful careers and we wanted to be the ones calling the shots. We decided that we would go ahead and fund the album ourselves. But then Richard Desmond, the owner of *OK!*, said that he would put up the money for recording the album and help with the publicity. We would have to pay him his costs back from the profit, but everything else would go to the charities. Richard is closely involved with several charities already, so he seemed like an ideal person. We also knew and liked him from our work with his magazine. And he's a shrewd businessman, so we knew it would be in his best interest to promote us as much as possible to help make the album a success so that he would get his money back and the charities would benefit.

We selected six charities, in the end. I chose Vision, a charity for blind and visually impaired children; Pete chose the NSPCC, because he is one of their ambassadors; and Richard Desmond and his wife chose the charities that they are involved with: The Moorfields Eye Hospital (The Richard Desmond Children's Eye Centre), the Disability Foundation, Norwood Children and Families First. It really didn't bother me that I wasn't going to be making any money from the album, because not only was it my dream come true to be able to sing the songs that I loved, I was also going to be helping these charities.

However, this deal didn't get signed until the

Autumn of 2006, which meant Pete and me were working on the album during the spring and summer before anything had been agreed and I couldn't help feeling pessimistic. *Here we go again,* I thought, *I'm back in the studio, but I haven't seen any contract. I don't believe this album is ever going to be released.* Because the promises people had made me in the past about my music have resulted in fuck all, I didn't believe that anything was actually going to happen until the contract had been signed and I saw my albums on sale. After a couple of months of working on our duets, I had a frank conversation with Claire, my manager. 'I'm not being funny,' I said, 'but I've been told I will get a record deal so many times in the past and, if you want to know the truth, I'm not that enthusiastic about going into the studio. I just don't want all this work to be for nothing.' She reassured me that there was definitely going to be a deal, that she wasn't bullshitting us.

But regardless of my doubts, I love singing and I enjoyed having my singing lessons. It was great singing with Pete too. I thought, even if no deal ever comes off, at least Pete and I will have an album of our favourite songs. Having said that, we agonised

over which ones to choose – there were just so many
I wanted to include! And at first there were several
songs that I hated – I didn't want to sing 'Islands in
the Stream', 'Cherish', 'Don't Go Breaking My Heart'
or 'I've Had the Time of My Life'. But Nicky and Deni
encouraged me to record them, telling me that I
would like them once we'd done them. Of course
there were songs that I loved as well – 'A Whole New
World' and 'Endless Love' were my favourites. There
were also three original songs that Pete helped write,
including 'Lullaby', 'I Come Down' and 'The Two
of Us'.

When we'd recorded all the songs, I really did like
the result, even the songs that I'd had my doubts
about. We decided to call the album *A Whole New
World*, as that song means so much to us. We'd sang
it at our wedding and, by a complete coincidence, it
was one of the songs playing on the radio when I had
Junior, so it's incredibly special to us. I loved the
whole recording experience. It gave me back my
confidence about singing and I loved working with
my husband, although we are chalk and cheese when
it comes to music. Pete is a complete perfectionist
and, over the months that we recorded our album,

fitting studio sessions around our other work, Pete would want to go back and re-record his vocals to get them spot on, whereas I'd be like, 'Okay, give me the words and I'll get on with it.' And I'd get in that booth, sing my heart out, then leave, thinking job done and not obsessing about whether I could have done such and such a line differently. I could probably record a song in three hours. I love singing and I want to get it right, but I'm not as obsessed or as passionate about it as Pete. For him, music is his life, whereas for me, it's something that I really enjoy doing, but I've also got a lot of other things I like to do as well. We did have words about it. His attitude was that, if I wasn't putting 100 per cent in, it would affect the song and it would affect him. 'Try your best,' he'd say. 'I'm involved in this as well and I really want the album to sound good.' And of course that's what I wanted as well, but I'm just not as anal about music as he is. His feelings about music are like mine about modelling and, when we do a shoot together, I'm the perfectionist and want to get every shot exactly how I want it, whereas Pete is more casual.

* * *

While we were working on the album, I was feeling so much better in myself. Yes, I did have moments when I felt sad about the miscarriage, but I also felt I'd moved on. I was still seeing my therapist and still taking a small dose of anti-depressant, but I felt in a completely different place to the beginning of the year when I had felt so low that I couldn't see a way out of my depression. As I was feeling so much happier, I decided that now was the perfect time to get my boobs done. I had already seen several surgeons and they'd all said that I should wait until I'd had all my children. But me being me, I didn't want to wait. I told Pete that if I didn't get pregnant in the next couple of months, I was going for my fourth boob job and that we'd have to wait a year or so before trying for another baby. I hated my boobs as they were – the implants were old and having two kids had made them sag – so I went ahead and booked myself in for an op. When it comes to boobs, I like the stuck-on look. Everyone knows I've got implants and I don't care if my boobs do look fake. In fact, I want them to look like that! I've never been one for the natural look, after all, but I wanted my boobs to be more pert and slightly smaller. Unfortunately, this meant I would end up with a keyhole scar that ran round the nipple and vertically down the breast – the scar would be visible, unlike the scars I have from previous operations, which are under my breasts. But it's not as if I do full-frontal topless modelling any-more, and, if I do, the pictures can just be airbrushed afterwards.

* * *

It was mid October and I was busy recording in the studio. I had a streaming cold, but by now the pressure was on us to finish the album, so I had to go ahead and record it anyway, and I think you can hear on 'The Two of Us' that I sound nasally. In spite of my cold and feeling generally a bit run down and nauseous (which I just put down to the cold), I was really excited, because I was booked in to get my new boobs in a couple of days and I couldn't wait! Because I had a cold, I was a bit concerned that they might not be able to go ahead with the operation, so I called the clinic to check that it was safe. I was told that it would be fine, but the nurse then asked me to confirm that I was definitely coming in, revealing that my manager had called them to see if there was any way that the surgeon could talk me out of having the op because I had so much work on and it would be better to postpone it until I had time to recover.

'Don't listen to her!' I insisted, 'I'll be okay.' I was determined to get my new boobs!

'You do know that you're going to have to rest after the operation,' the nurse carried on.

'Yeah, yeah,' I replied casually. 'I'm only singing at the moment, I don't have to dance yet. I've had three boob jobs, so I know what to expect.' And I thought, *I'm having them done and that's final!* And I was so excited at the thought. I suppose it was a bit cheeky of my management to call the clinic, but they were right to be concerned. I did have a lot of work on and you do need recovery time after surgery.

Nicola was filming me for our TV series as I made the call and, when I came off the phone, I turned to the camera and said, 'My management can say what they like, but I'm getting my boobs done tomorrow. There's only one thing in the world that would stop me and that would be if I was pregnant. Just to prove that I'm not, I'm going to do a test right now!' So I grabbed my bag and said on camera, 'Right, I'm just going for a wee,' and went off to the ladies. I was completely confident that the test would come back negative and totally unprepared for the result. *No fucking way!* I thought, staring in astonishment at the strong blue line appearing on the predictor kit. *It's positive!* I opened the cubicle door and held up the test for Nicola to film. 'You're not going to believe this,' I said, keeping my voice down, as there were people in the studio next door and I didn't want them to hear my news, 'but I'm pregnant!' I couldn't believe it. For a minute I wondered if the test was showing up positive because of my miscarriage and that maybe I still had pregnancy hormones in my system. But then I reasoned that that happened months ago, so it couldn't be. I was pregnant and this explained why I'd been feeling a bit sick for the past couple of days.

I had a shoot to do after the recording at a photographer's studio nearby. Pete was meeting me there and I couldn't wait to tell him the news. As soon as he arrived, I said, 'Pete, I've got something to tell you and I don't know what you're going to feel about it.'

He looked worried and said, 'What?' And then I held the test in front of him and he exclaimed, 'Oh my God, no way!' and then we were hugging and kissing and we were both so excited. Our song 'A Whole New World' was in the background as I'd wanted to play it to the photographer, not because I love the sound of my own voice! So that made the song even more special for us; it was a sweet moment, just as it had been when the song played as I had Junior. We hadn't been trying for another baby, but I suppose we hadn't exactly been careful either, thinking that if it happened, it happened. It was only four months since my miscarriage and I worried that I'd got pregnant too quickly, as the doctors had advised us to wait at least three months before trying again. But, in spite of these worries, I was very happy. I wanted another baby more than anything.

*   *   *

Within a few days, morning sickness kicked in with a vengeance – except I don't know why they call it morning sickness, because I felt nauseous and was sick all through the day. I felt awful. I was off my food. There was nothing that I wanted to eat and that made me feel even sicker. I'd suffered from morning sickness when I was pregnant with Junior, but nothing like this, this was the worst. All I wanted to do was crawl into bed until I felt better. But finally the contracts had been signed and so the album was definitely being released and in just a few weeks we had a hectic publicity campaign to promote it. Talk about bad timing. It seemed that every time I had something big lined up to do with my singing I was pregnant and therefore not feeling my best. When I took part in the Eurovision show, I was five months pregnant and felt crap and now here I was about to launch my album – something that had been my dream for as long as I could remember – and I was pregnant. My emotions were all over the place as well and, while I was thrilled to be pregnant, I was also terrified of having another miscarriage. I didn't think I could bear to have another one – it was so upsetting. It was a relief when we had the first scan and saw the tiny baby and heard the heart beat, but I knew I had a long way to go. I often found myself saying 'Please be all right' to the baby in the months that followed.

* * *

Before our album was released – before anyone had even heard one of the songs – we had people slating us and taking the piss. A supposed recording of Pete and me singing 'A Whole New World' even came out on the Internet. Pete heard it and he just said that it was someone mucking about, that it was a stitch-up, as the song had obviously been tampered with to make my voice sound flat. *How pathetic is that?* I thought. *We're releasing this album for charity, not to make money for ourselves.* I put it out of my mind. If I worried about what anyone thought, I'd never do anything. The fact is, there'll always be someone who'll make a joke about us because they don't want Pete and me to do well.

The album was going to be released at the end of November, followed by our single 'A Whole New World'. We filmed the video for the single in Venice, which was perfect, as Pete had taken me there on a surprise romantic weekend just before I had Junior and it will always have happy memories for me. The whole look of the video, which was in black and white, was inspired by the famous 1950s Italian film *La Dolce Vita* which means 'The Sweet Life', but don't ask me to tell you any more as I've never seen the film, I just know it's a classic. The idea for the video had been Claire's and I think it was a really good one. In my last autobiography I know I criticised her over Eurovision and the music deal that she'd promised me and I know I upset her, but that's how I felt about what had happened. But my relationship with her has changed since then, and now, if I've got a problem with something, I come out with it.

It was great making the video and dressing up in some gorgeous dresses – including a full-length red number with a corset top and a huge sweeping skirt, which I loved wearing. I almost wished I'd got my wedding dress from the same designers, Hollywood Dreams, because I loved it so much. However, I did have a good old moan about my hair, which for some parts had to be styled in a fifties style, shoulder length and curled. I have *very* strong views about how my hair should look, but when I saw the film back I realised that it worked perfectly. And it was fun acting the part of a 1950s film star – all those shots of Pete and me exchanging sultry, longing looks at each other; dressing up in another fabulous dress for a masked ball and then being pursued by the press and driving away in a cool vintage sports car with Pete. The ending was so sweet, with Pete walking towards me holding a heart-shaped balloon with *Will you marry me?* written on it, and in the background was the statue of an angel and, for a second, Pete stood in front of it and he looked as if he had wings, as if he was an angel.

The video only took two days to film, which was a major bonus for me. I'm a very impatient person and I hate sitting around. Whenever I'm posing for photographs, I'll say to the photographer, 'Have you got the shot then? Right, on to the next one.' I get bored so quickly and I know when they've got the shot. But luckily the director on the video shoot was very speedy and I didn't have the chance to get bored. The only downside to the video shoot was that I kept being sick and I was exhausted. How was I going to cope promoting the album over the next two months?

* * *

'Oh God, I think I'm going to be sick again!' I exclaimed, and Pete had to quickly hand me yet another plastic bag. This was becoming an all-too familiar scenario whenever I got in the car to go anywhere and on this day, of all days, I could have done without it. We were travelling up to Blackpool to a gay club to do our first PA to promote the album and, as well as the morning sickness, I felt sick with nerves at the thought of singing live. Although we had recorded the songs, I didn't yet know them off by heart and I just didn't know if I was confident enough to go on stage and perform them. Just the thought of it was bringing back memories of Eurovision and of how nervous I'd been then. I was convinced that I'd forget all the words and that I wouldn't be able to sing a note.

I hadn't done a club appearance for ages, not while I'd been with Pete, so we're talking over two years. I used to do them regularly, before I got fed up of being shouted at to get my tits out by drunk clubbers and because I didn't like being away from Harvey for the night. Back then, I'd always have a few drinks first to calm my nerves and give me confidence, as it's pretty intimidating going on stage in front of a packed audience of pissed clubbers, I can tell you. But there was no chance of that now I was pregnant and the very thought of alcohol made me want to throw up, so I was going to have to go on stage stone-cold sober, sing and look confident. The thought was terrifying. I didn't know if I could do it and I was shitting myself with nerves. As Gary got to work on my make-up, I tried not to think about what was coming up. I wanted to look sexy, even though I felt like shit, and so he gave me the smoky-eyed vampy look that I like. I also dressed in black because I felt fat, even though I wasn't, because I was only a few weeks gone, but I always feel big once I know I'm pregnant. I was wearing hot pants, a tight T-shirt, fishnets and black high heels. Just before we went on stage, I checked myself in the mirror, taking a few deep breaths and trying to pull myself together, telling myself that I could do it. Pete was brilliant, reassuring me, telling me that I would be fine, that I should just enjoy it, but as we waited to go on, I really didn't know if I could do it. I felt sick, I had butterflies, I couldn't keep still because of my nerves. I could not wait for it to be over. I had a little peep through a gap in the curtains and I could see the crowd; that freaked me out even more and I thought, *Oh no! I'm going to have a panic attack!*

Then the first notes of 'The Best Things In Life Are Free' started up and I had to walk down one flight of stairs onto the stage and Pete had to walk down the other. There was no turning back now. The crowd were cheering and screaming their appreciation. And it wouldn't have mattered if I hadn't sung a single note, the crowd carried on screaming and whistling throughout the song and I doubt they could hear anything, as they just seemed happy to see us on stage. After I'd got the first number out of the way, I said, 'Hi, I just want you to know that this is my first singing PA, so bear with me if I look a bit stiff!' And they all cheered again. After that, I felt slightly more confident as we sang 'A Whole New World', followed by 'Don't Go Breaking My Heart' and ending with 'The Two of Us'. That was to become our set for the rest of our PAs.

It was such a relief to get the PA out of the way, but I didn't feel like celebrating, as I felt so knackered and sick from my pregnancy. I know I sound like I'm moaning, but I really did feel rough. And not only was I feeling sick, but it was also bloody freezing outside and I couldn't wait to get the high heels off, take my make-up off and get into bed. It was so cold in my hotel room that I had to wear my dressing gown to bed, so not exactly a rock and roll moment . . . And as I lay in bed trying to warm up, I had a sick feeling in my gut as I realised that this was only the first of many PAs – never mind the Royal Variety

Performance at the beginning of December, which I couldn't even bear to think about.

I tried to stay calm but, as the publicity campaign got underway, I felt horribly under pressure, especially about the PAs, because there were so many booked in. I just didn't know if I could cope. I felt so unwell with my pregnancy, plus I had all the added pressure that no one knew I was pregnant and it was a strain pretending that I was okay. Of course all this publicity was going to be great for the album, but I couldn't help feeling that the campaign was too rushed. I felt that whenever plans were made around my singing career, it's never quite as organised and smooth as it should be. With Eurovision, I felt as if I was chucked in at the deep end and expected to sing live on TV with hardly any preparation. And I couldn't enjoy performing the song one little bit; if anything, I'd hated the experience. And now I was starting to get the same feeling about doing the PAs to promote our album. I just didn't feel prepared. Believe me, I can go on stage and model in my under-wear and I couldn't give a shit how many people are there, because I'm so confident in my modelling, but to sing and dance (because I'm not the greatest dancer) is a really big pressure. Pete's a great dancer and so we'd choreographed some moves where he worked around me and I'd just wiggle into him, but the only song we'd actually rehearsed and where I felt confident about moving around the stage was 'The Best Things In Life Are Free'.

There was also no budget for clothes, make-up, hairdressers or even cars to take us to the different venues. Usually, if you're with a record company, they would take care of everything, but because this album was for charity, Pete and me had to pay for everything ourselves and we wouldn't get any of the money back. I didn't mind that, but I hated feeling so rushed the whole time. Our management tried to get us on as many TV shows and radio stations as possible and it felt like we were constantly having to race here, there and everywhere. I'd have to do interviews or signings all day and then perform late at night, often after midnight. It would have been hard work even if I hadn't been pregnant. I just didn't feel that I was given enough time in the hectic schedule to get ready for the shows I was appearing on. I imagine that other singers have at least three hours to get ready before a performance, but with me there was hardly any time allowed for my make-up. As for my hair, I've got extensions, so I can't wash and blow dry it myself and there was never any time for me to get it done. There's only two people – Danielle and Melodie – who can blow dry my hair the way I like it anyway and so, when it needed washing, I had to tie it back in a ponytail instead and that meant I didn't feel that I looked my best. Our sunbed broke too, so I couldn't top up my tan, and I was getting paler and paler. I always think that you feel better when you've got some colour, even if you don't feel as good as you look. I thought my clothes didn't look right either, because I was so pale. I was also barely eating, because of the morning sickness, so my face looked gaunt. All in all, I felt and looked like shit, and when you feel like that it does affect your confidence when you come to perform. I told my manager exactly how I felt: 'At the end of the day, I'm the one who has to get up on stage in front of all those people. Whenever someone like Jennifer Lopez goes on stage she looks immaculate and that's what I want to look like, I want to look my absolute best. But I'm not and I'm having to pay for all my own outfits and there's got to be a bit of give and take. Imagine if I didn't have the money to pay for them. What then?'

'Well,' she replied, 'That's what the music industry is like, you have to expect these kinds of schedules.'

'Hang on a minute,' I shot back, 'you've thrown me in at the deep end. None of you seem to understand that I'm new to all this – I've only sung live a few times and now I'm expected to sing live and dance and I'm just not used to it, you've got to bear with me. And I'm not looking my best because everything is such a rush and no one is putting in enough time to make me feel good about myself. And whenever I'm in the car travelling to PAs, I should be resting, but you're making me do radio interviews. I never have a moment to myself. We're doing this for charity – we should be enjoying the moment. It's different if you're doing it to earn money for yourselves.'

Pete understood how I felt and he could see that I didn't have enough time in the busy schedule to get ready for our performances. Don't get me wrong, making the album for charity was brilliant, but the whole experience of promoting it was just not how I thought it would be. When I do something, I like to do it well. The next time we do an album – and I'm determined to – I want it be promoted in a way that I will actually enjoy.

The night we performed at the London nightclub GAY was a typical example of where things went wrong. The outfit I was supposed to be wearing was being flown over from Italy, but for some reason it was stopped at customs, so I couldn't get it in time. So Kerrie-Ann, my stylist, had to quickly find me a back-up dress – which ended up being a short tutu-style number. Because I was so white, I also asked her to find me some dance tights to cover up my pale legs. I then had an argument with Claire about what to wear under the tights. I was all for wearing a thong and it wasn't like I was flashing anything, as I was wearing tights, but Claire insisted that I wear something less revealing – a pair of shorts, in fact. When I said that it looked awful like that, she said that I had to have the Katie Price look to promote the album, not Jordan. I thought I looked crap and so unsexy and, because of that, I didn't enjoy performing on stage, even though the crowd gave us a great reception again. Though there were some real highlights during this time – *Children in Need* and

The Royal Variety Performance, for instance – there were some real low points too.

On 12 November 2006, Pete and me performed at the Radio 1 Chart Show at Brighton Dome, along with Beyoncé, Girls Aloud, McFly and Nelly Furtado, which should have been a great opportunity for us to promote the album. But yet again it was a rush to get there and for me to get ready. The photographs of me at that event are the shittiest ever as a result. I look awful. And of course I was feeling sick. But we wanted to do the gig as we thought it would be great publicity for the album. Wrong. We felt totally stitched up. We weren't singing live, thank God, and, as the music started, we went on stage and took our positions in front of the curtains. I kept expecting the curtains to open and allow us to take the full stage, but instead they remained shut, which only gave us about two foot to move in. Because we were performing 'A Whole New World', I was wearing a long, flowing white dress, because the theme is a fairy-tale one and I'm supposed to look like a princess, albeit a princess who needs a hair wash . . . and it wasn't easy manoeuvring the dress in the tiny space. Pete tried to walk up and down as he usually does during the song, which left me standing there trying to lip sync and feeling extremely self-conscious. Meanwhile, from behind the curtains the next band were warming up and you could clearly hear drums and guitars. I was fucking fuming. I felt like the organisers had humiliated us by inviting us to perform and then treating us as if we were a joke. But however angry we both felt, we kept it together, ignored the background noise and acted like it was cool, that we could work through anything. And while I felt humiliated by the experience and some of the other bands (I can't tell you who they were, because I don't even know!) were disrespectful to us, the audience were lovely. Yes, our music was different to every other band and singer playing – we were performing a Disney number – but while they were laughing at us they should have remembered that we were doing it for charity.

I was also annoyed by the way some radio stations covered the launch of our album. It seemed that they were all too happy to use Pete and me for publicity, and I'd hear the DJs bigging it up about how they had an interview with us to get listeners in, yet they wouldn't play our song. They obviously thought that

Despite all that has happened to us, Pete and I are as strong as ever.

With Pete's brother Mike in Cyprus.

We had a lovely
night out with
Pete's parents
Savva and Thea.

Pete's brother
Chris performing.

Happy after a fun night.

My boys.

Watching a film in the
cinema at home with popcorn.

Taking a break from my hectic
work schedule.

we weren't credible artists and, therefore, they wouldn't play it. I almost felt like saying, 'Well don't interview me then, because if you're not going to bother to play our song, that's out of order.' But I tell you now I will never forget who didn't play it . . . I also thought, *This is for charity, why won't you make an exception? You should be helping to promote this album because it's going to benefit so many people.* It was very disappointing. The stations would usually play a really short burst of our song or some stations would do their own spoof versions of it. Chris Moyles, in particular, wouldn't actually play the song and he recorded his own parody version and just ripped the piss out of ours. I know Pete and me are never going to be considered as credible by some people in the music industry no matter what we do, because they just don't want us to be, but the fact is, I don't know anyone else who has dedicated their whole album to charity out of their own pocket. I don't think people realise the time and effort it took to produce and promote the album. It really pissed me off that no one even picked up on all the hard work that had gone into it – it didn't just appear overnight.

* * *

Just a few days after the Radio 1 Show, Pete and I were presenting a gong at the World Music Awards and we were both really excited – Pete especially so, because Michael Jackson was going to be there and he's one of his music icons. I had found the most amazing dress to wear – a white number with a crystal-encrusted bodice revealing just enough cleavage and a skirt that was short at the front and then flowing at the back, like a wedding-dress train. As soon as I tried it on, I couldn't wait to wear it. In contrast to how I'd been feeling about my appearance lately, I felt so good about how I looked on the night of the awards. I loved my hair and my make-up and felt really confident. There was a massive red carpet leading up to the venue, which was in Earls Court, and the place was packed with press and photographers. It was a huge press call – I don't think I've seen so many photographers before. Because there were so many stars from the music industry there, I didn't think Pete and me would get any attention – in fact, because it was press from around the world, I didn't even think they would know who we were. But as we walked up the carpet the cameras clicked away at us and we did get interviewed. I felt really proud as the crowds looked on, and thought, *So people do know who we are!* It was a real confidence boost. Later in the evening, when we presented the award for the World's Best New Artist to James Blunt, I got another boost when we walked on stage and received one of the loudest cheers of the night. It's at moments like these that I feel proudest, because whatever some people in the music industry think, the public like us. And that's when I get my revenge on all those people who put us down, because they can say what they like, but when we're at an event we always get the biggest cheers.

While I enjoyed the awards, I didn't like being surrounded by so many people who were so full of their own self-importance or who were – to put it plainly – up their own arse. Several of these types came up to me that night, giving me all this chat, saying, 'Wow, you look amazing!' and then they'd ask if I'd be interested in promoting this or that. I'd smile and say, 'Just give the details to my manager.' I know from experience that none of them ever follow it up, they're just bullshitters and I can't bear it. As we were leaving, I met Paris Hilton and we got talking. She might not be everyone's cup of tea, but I've always liked her for her style. She knew who I was and wanted a picture of us together on her camera phone, and I took one with mine too. After that we texted each other every now and then and arranged to meet up and go shopping together when I went to LA to promote my TV series. But I don't go on about my friendship with her in the press because I'm not a name dropper and I don't need to do that to get publicity . . .

At the end of November, Pete and I performed on *Children In Need* again, singing 'The Best Things In Life Are Free', and that was such a positive experience for me. I was proud to be singing for such a good cause and I felt confident with the song and with my dance moves. I'd appeared on *Children In Need* the year before, so I was familiar with the format of the show and the set-up. I'd also had plenty of time to get ready and felt I looked good. But the other performances were getting too much for me. I didn't have a minute to myself. I was under pressure, stressed and these feelings were made so much worse because I was pregnant. I was becoming worried about the baby, worried that the stress might trigger a miscarriage. In the past I had bottled things up and not been upfront with my management about how I'd felt, but this time I said what I thought. 'Claire,' I said, after another gruelling day, 'I'm not going to lose this baby because I'm so stressed. I don't know if I can go on working like this.' I was starting to feel like I had at the beginning of the year when my Postnatal Depression was at its worst. But I didn't get the response I wanted, as Claire replied, 'You have to, we have to make this album work.'

In the end I managed five PAs in total and then I had to say to Claire, 'Look, the club PAs are just too much for me. I can't do them anymore, I'm burning myself out.' And it was true — I was absolutely knackered. My body was saying it was too much. And I wasn't seeing the boys enough and I really missed them. I told Claire, 'I've got kids and we're doing this for charity, it's not as if this is my only career. I'm not interested in what it's like for other bands, they haven't got kids, or homes to run. They probably stay in hotels and they can cope with late nights because they haven't got to get up first thing in the morning with children like I have to.' The bottom line was that

I've always said that I want to enjoy my work and my music and I just wasn't enjoying this.

We did have an appearance coming up that I would never have cancelled in a million years, though – appearing on the Royal Variety Performance. When Claire revealed that Pete and me had been asked to go on it to sing 'A Whole New World', I was well excited. 'That's brilliant!' I said. 'Whoever would have thought that *I* would get to go on stage and sing in front of Prince Charles!' I couldn't help thinking that I'd come a long way since my Page 3 days. When I remembered all the negative things that had been said about me, I thought, *Up yours to everyone who has knocked me!* But I was slightly pissed off when I discovered that, while the organisers wanted us on the show, they were only allowing us to sing one verse. But then I thought, *At least we're on it, and that's all that matters.* But in the run up to the show, my nerves were so bad and, as usual, I was thinking that there was no way I could go on stage in front of so many people. On the day of the show, 5 December, we had to rehearse with all the other acts and we were going to be backed by a full-scale orchestra who were going to be playing in a different key to the one

I was used to. Because I'm not a professional singer, and I've never pretended to be, it's not easy to change the key to a song once I'm used to it. Worse still, the key they were playing in was higher. I was incredibly nervous about singing in the Royal Albert Hall, which is a huge venue, and there'd be an audience of thousands, plus it was going to be on TV. I had flashbacks to Eurovision again. During the rehearsals I felt more and more uptight – all the other performers were either professional singers or actors and they were all very straight-faced, taking everything very seriously; there was no one to have a laugh with and I thought, *Fucking hell! I'm not used to being with people like this!* I was also given a mic during rehearsal that I wasn't familiar with and, when I asked if it could be turned up, I was told that I would have to hold it closer to my mouth, which threw me, because I've never been taught to sing using a mic properly. At least there was one thing that I was confident about and that was my outfit. I was wearing the most gorgeous white dress by Isabell Kristensen, the same designer who created my wedding dress. It had a sparkling ivory bodice with layers upon layers of white netting as the skirt. When we'd finished our rehearsal, we appeared on the Paul O'Grady Show. I don't get nervous anymore about appearing on TV chat shows, but that day I had such butterflies because all I could think of was how, in a few hours' time, I was going to be singing on The Royal Variety Performance. I couldn't help feeling that some people were waiting for us to fuck up.

Before the show, the acts met Prince Charles and Camilla, and I was actually quite nervous. I don't normally give a shit who anyone is, I just try and be myself, but I think, because we were all standing in a line waiting to meet him, the feeling of anticipation from everyone else rubbed off on me. When he arrived, everyone was in awe and it hit me what a special moment this was. Prince Charles was nice and asked if we were singing. And then I said to Camilla, 'That's a nice frock you're wearing,' and I thought, *Where the hell did I get that word from? I never say frock – what a dickhead I am!* She seemed really nice, though, and said that she'd watched us get together in the jungle. I didn't ask her what she'd thought of Pete's stonker when he'd crept out of my sleeping bag after having a cuddle with me, mind you. Even I know where to draw the line . . . But, to me, better than meeting royalty was the fact that Pete and me were in the line up beside Take That and it was such an honour, because when I was younger I was such a huge fan. They're all such lovely guys as well.

We had our own tiny dressing room at the Albert Hall and we couldn't hear the show, as it's such a massive venue and our dressing room was miles away from the stage. Five minutes before our song, we had to wait backstage, Pete on one side of the stage, me on the other, and I could see the packed auditorium. *Holy Fucking Shit, I can't get out of this one!* I thought, and then I panicked. *Oh my God, I can't do this!* I felt under such pressure to do well. I turned round to Nicola, who was with me, and said, 'I can't do it!' and she was trying to calm me down, saying 'Yes you can.' As the orchestra struck up the notes of our song, I felt so exposed as I walked onto the stage. I tried to tell myself not to worry and to just concentrate on singing, because I was petrified that I'd open my mouth and only a squeak would come out – and how shameful would that have been in front of millions of viewers? Straightaway I was slightly thrown because of the high key, but because we only had one verse and it was going to be over so quickly, I had to get it right. I did it. I sang as well as I could and hopefully showed people I can actually sing. I was shitting myself, though, and it was such a massive relief when it was all over. Pete was disappointed, as he thought he'd performed better in the rehearsal, but all I could think of was that it was over!

Overall, the Royal Variety Performance felt like a real achievement and it was great that we could be on such a high-profile show. Best of all, whatever some people might have thought, the album did well when it was released on 27 November. Some record companies thought we wouldn't even sell ten thousand copies, so when we went straight into the charts at number twenty in the first week, it must have surprised a lot of people in the music industry and made them want to eat their words. And when the single of 'A Whole New World' was released, it went in at number ten. We ended up selling over a hundred and ninety thousand albums and it went platinum, which I don't think is at all bad. After some of the record companies saw how well the album did, they wanted to sign us up, and that's when I got my revenge by turning them down, thinking, *No Way!*

You didn't want to know us in the beginning. You'd only offer us a measly advance. You wanted to control us, and didn't think we'd sell any albums, so bollocks to you because we don't need you! Pete and me are definitely going to do another album together now where we'll have solo numbers as well. And then my ambition is to bring out my own solo album and Pete would like to do his, but we're not in a rush, because we have so many other projects on the go. Looking back, I'm so pleased we did the album. But all the time I was promoting it I was so worried that I might lose the baby, through stress, or that I'd get Postnatal Depression again, so it just wasn't the fun experience it might have been . . . Better luck next time, I hope.

CHAPTER TEN

GIRLS JUST WANNA HAVE FUN

Every now and then during my pregnancy I'd tell Pete that, as soon as the baby was born, I was going to let my hair down, have a few drinks and go clubbing. And he would say that was fine and that he didn't mind, but deep down I knew that he did, because it's been a real issue between us in the past. We have so much in common and are close in every way, but when it comes to this, we do not see eye to eye at all. Pete doesn't understand how, every now and then, I would like to be able to go out clubbing with my girlfriends and have a drink and a laugh. I definitely haven't got a drink problem. In the four years we've been together, I've probably only been drunk five or six times, but on the rare occasion that I've got pissed, Pete makes it feel like I do have a problem and he turns it into such a big deal. He worries that, when I'm drunk, I could end up being unfaithful, but that's crap. He's just remembering his own past when he went out clubbing. 'I know what drunk girls are like, Kate,' he tells me, 'I know how easy they are.'

'It doesn't mean that *I* am easy, Pete!' I reply. 'Just because you were able to get into those girls' knickers doesn't mean that other men can do that to me! I'm definitely not the kind of girl who, once they've had a drink, will open their legs at quarter to three!' It just goes to show what kinds of slags he went for in the past . . . I know, however off my head I was, in my wildest moment, that I wouldn't want to kiss or shag another bloke. I just want to have a laugh with my friends, get pissed and have a dance – it's as simple as that. Pete hates what I'm like when I've had a drink. He tells me that my personality completely changes. But who doesn't change when they have a drink? That's the whole point, isn't it? To get a bit merry, to get that nice relaxed feeling. I become more confident and I love it. The fact is, I get paranoid that people are staring at me when I go out and I feel I can't let my guard down. When I've had a couple of cocktails, I relax and forget about the stares.

I'm not into drinking at home, though. I'm not the kind of person who comes back after work and has a glass of wine, or who even goes out to the pub and has a drink, as I just don't see the point of that. No, I like having a drink on a big night out, and it's about the whole package for me – getting ready with my girlfriends, gossiping, laughing, listening to music, deciding what to wear, drinking our Bacardi Breezers; then going to the club, having cocktails and getting just drunk enough to have the confidence to hit the dance floor and not be self-conscious. I know I'm not much of a dancer, and when I'm sober I feel too awkward, but with a few drinks inside me I feel as if I've got the moves and I let rip.

Whenever we talk about me wanting to go out with my friends, Pete winds me up by saying that, if I'm going to go out with my friends, then he's going to go out with his. But the fact is he hates clubs and it pisses me off that he's only saying he'll go out as a threat. When he used to go out clubbing and pull women, he was stone-cold sober and it's worse to me knowing that you can be sober and still be that confident! I only want to go out once every month or two and I think it's perfectly normal. But Pete tries to make out that I'm in the wrong for wanting to, that it isn't normal. And it's bollocks! Everyone's entitled to have a night out every now and then. You only live once and, before I know it, I'll be bloody forty and then it'll be too late for me to go out clubbing with my girlfriends. Sometimes I feel I'm made to be old before my time.

I'm not saying that I blame Pete for the night I ended up taking drugs during my lowest suffering from the Postnatal Depression, that's my responsibility alone. But a small part of me feels that Pete drove me to that point because he's so against me having a drink and having any kind of release. I know that my depression would not have been cured by getting pissed; all I'm saying is that, if I'd had a drink, I might not have ended up doing what I did that night. I feel like saying to Pete, *If only you would let me drink without giving me such aggro about it, without making me feel guilty.* But the fact is that the few times in our marriage that I've got drunk we've nearly split up over it.

Whenever Pete and I go out together, I usually drink diet coke and I can't help thinking to myself, *I'm a mum of three and I've got a career, but I'm only 29 – why can't I let my hair down?* My mum's in her fifties and yet she goes out every weekend with her girlfriends, my dad goes out with his friends and they'll meet up at the end of the night, and it's the same with my brother and his wife. It's the way I've been brought up, it's normal and I fucking hate the fact that it has become such an issue between Pete and me. I always promised my sister Sophie that, when she was old enough, I would take her out to some of the London clubs, but I just don't know if I can stand the arguments that will follow if I do.

Pete won't ever let himself get drunk, because he had a severe panic attack once when he was drunk and he was terrified that he was going to die. I do sympathise, but I also think he needs to chill out about me wanting to have a drink. In his autobiography he's got a whole chapter talking about how much he hates me drinking – detailing every single time that I've got drunk in our relationship, and the fact that he can name every one of them proves how rarely it has happened. He specifically talked about the night we went to the glamorous Chinese New Year party thrown by the socialite Andy Wong and his wife Patti in January 2006. Now, I admit I was out to have a good time. I was wearing a figure-hugging sheer black and silver dress, which didn't leave much to the imagination. Well, what the hell, I felt like I deserved to have a good time – the past few months had been so shit. At first I felt self-conscious at the party, as I hardly knew anyone, so I just talked to Pete, but then Rebecca Loos came over to us and introduced herself and we all got chatting. I annoyed Pete because every time I had another drink I'd say, 'I'm definitely not going to get drunk,' when really I knew I was and I admit I did get pissed. According to Pete – I can't remember – Rebecca told him that she thought I had an amazing body and would love to touch it. Well in your dreams, sunshine, is all I can say! I'm sure she was just saying it to wind Pete up. Anyway, Rebecca and me ended up going to the ladies together – no, not because I fancied a bit of girl-on-girl action – and I got talking to some of the other girls in there about the usual girlie things, like hair and outfits. I was probably in there for fifteen minutes at the most, but in Pete's mind it was half an hour and he was seriously starting to wonder what I was getting up to. Well, a big fat nothing is the answer and I can't believe he would think I would even consider doing anything with Rebecca Loos – I mean a) I'm not into girls at all and b) even if I was, I wouldn't choose her unless I wanted the whole world to know! For the rest of the night I went off and chatted to other people with the confidence the drinks had given me, ignoring Pete, and that wound him up as well. He's not the only man I've been with who's had a problem with me doing this. Every man I've ever had a relationship with has got the hump about it, but I don't do it on purpose.

Another time, I went clubbing with my friends – I can remember the exact month, March 2006, which shows what a rare event it was. Pete had a PA at a club somewhere and I had planned to go out in Brighton with some girlfriends, including my friend Rachel and Kerrie-Ann, my stylist. However, when we phoned round the Brighton clubs, we found out that none of them had any tables we could reserve or any secure areas where I could hang out with my friends and not be surrounded by people wanting autographs and taking pictures. 'Fuck it,' I said, 'Let's go to London.' I knew that in a London club they'd look after me and make sure I wasn't hassled. It's not that I'm being arsey about mixing with people, it's just that this was a night out, it wasn't work, and I wanted to chill.

I didn't bother telling Pete that we were going to London; there seemed no point as he knew I was going out and what did a difference in location mean? We had such a great night. I got Rob, the driver we often use, to drive us to London and, on the way, we were listening to eighties music and singing along and drinking Bacardi Breezers. At The Embassy, I had a real laugh with the girls, drinking and dancing. It was just what I needed. But the next day, when Pete discovered I'd been out in London and that I hadn't told him, we had a massive row. The row lasted three days, it was so bad. He claimed that he was hurt that I hadn't phoned him to let him know that I was going to The Embassy, but I really couldn't see what his problem was.

'It's much better for you if I go out in London,' I told him, 'Because if I did get up to anything – not that I ever would – you'd hear about it straightaway in the press. And, anyway, I don't want to go out and flirt, to get anyone's number or shag anyone! I just want to go out and have a drink and a laugh.' *Fucking hell*, I thought, *Am I going to get this every time I go out?'* I don't like his attitude and it does piss me off. There's a gremlin inside me and I worry that one day it will explode and I'll end up shouting at Pete, 'Do you know what? I am fucking going out and, if you don't like it, then you can fucking go!' Pete made such a big deal of me wanting to go out that it reached a point where I didn't bother going out because I couldn't stand the arguments, but I don't think that's good for me. And Pete should realise that I've changed so much for him. Before I met him I went out all the time with my mates, now I rarely go out and, while I'm happy at home with the kids, having friends over for dinner or watching movies together in our cinema room, I do miss that buzz you get from a night out. There's no point thinking I could go out with my friends and not drink, though, either, because they'd all be pissed and I'd be sitting there like Miss Quiet and I'd never be able to dance without a drink inside me.

Pete also got angry with me for having a drink when he was away for a night doing a gig. I think the reason was more to do with his insecurities, though. I had my friend Sally over to the house and, after a few drinks, I thought it would be a great idea to order a cab and see my friend Neil, who lives nearby, and go out clubbing in Brighton. Neil is a really good friend who I've known since I was fourteen, but we've never dated, even though, when I was fourteen, I really fancied him. We've always been great mates and would go out together in a group with his girlfriend. But nothing has ever happened between us, even though lots of my friends apparently thought we would end up together. I rang Pete and told him what we planned to do, but he was furious, telling me no way should I go and see Neil. He's a personal trainer, so I can't lie and say he hasn't got a fit body, because he has, and that's what Pete's problem was. He can be insecure about his own body, even though I love it. He was worried about me seeing a bloke with a fit body when I'd had a few drinks. Believe me, if something was going to happen between me and

Neil, it would have happened years ago – we are just friends. But, as it turned out, Sally and me were perfectly happy to stay at my house. At some point I went out to the garage to get more wine and, when I was outside, Pete called. When I didn't answer, he thought I must have left or invited Neil over. The following morning Pete came home and had a real go at me, interrogating me about what I'd been up to. 'If you don't believe me, check the security cameras!' I told him, knowing that I had absolutely nothing to hide, 'And you'll see that I didn't go anywhere and that no one came here.' So he did and he quickly realised that I was telling the truth and he apologised.

On one occasion where I did have a drink at home, we were rehearsing our duets in the studio in front of my sister and I ended up opening a bottle of wine to make me feel more relaxed about singing. I'm such a light-weight when it comes to alcohol that, after a few glasses, I was pissed, but we were all having a laugh, so I didn't think it mattered. When Pete and I were on our own, I told him I was going to take him to the stables and shag him – as you do when you've had too much to drink and are feeling raunchy. Anyway, the next day, just because I couldn't remember every single detail of what we'd got up to, he threw it back in my face. 'I can't believe you can't remember!' he exclaimed. 'How do you expect me to trust that you know what you're doing when you go out and get drunk?'

'For fuck's sake, Pete,' I snapped back, 'I know full well when to say no, I always have done. However pissed I am, I'd know if someone's going to stick their dick in me!'

Sometimes when I'm in the car on my own and I've got my music on, I think I'd love to go out tonight. But then I think, I can't, because it will cause too much grief between Pete and me and it does put a downer on me. I know that when you're with someone you do have to compromise sometimes, and I have done over lots of things, all I ask is to be able to go out with my friends once in a while. There has been some progress, though. Pete ended up seeing my therapist and she helped him understand that I don't have a drink problem and that he's the one who has a problem over me having a drink and that's something for him to deal with. So we'll just have to see what happens. Pete's probably going to read this chapter and say, 'Just go out then! I didn't realise you felt like this.' But I have told him how I feel. I suppose I'm the rebellious type and, if I'm told I can't do something, it makes me want to do it even more. If Pete said, 'Go on then, go out clubbing.' I probably wouldn't even be that interested!

CHAPTER ELEVEN

KATIE PRICE MEANS BUSINESS

Whenever I have to fill out forms and I have to state my occupation, I always wonder which one to put down – model, singer, TV presenter or author? I always end up writing model – though the reality is that I do so many other things now. I hardly ever model anymore and I think the whole glamour industry has changed. It's not like it used to be. The lads mags, like *FHM* and *Loaded*, seem to put any girl on their covers these days. Whereas, when my career mainly centred on glamour modelling, it was a really big deal to be on the cover and showed that you were the top of the glamour girls. But I still want to continue with my glamour modelling – even more so when I've had my boobs done. I think I'm actually slimmer than I was before I had children, though I do need to tone. Mind you, I've always said that! And when I say glamour modelling, I don't mean the kind of Page 3 shoots that I did years ago. I've been there, done that and what would I gain from doing a stand there, tits out shoot? Glamour modelling isn't just about posing topless. What inspires me are the sexy, stylish glamour shoots, where it's all about the pose and looking provocative. I'd still pose completely naked if I was perhaps being photographed from the side, with my boobs covered, though, and I'm even considering posing for *American Playboy* again. I loved the original shoot I did for that magazine in 2002. I did reveal more than I ever had before, including my pink love heart tattoo where you'd normally have a Brazilian. But I thought the pictures were erotic rather than pornographic. Put it this way, I'd never pose with my legs at quarter to three. Never have done and never will. I told my manager that, now my Katie Price career is really established and is totally separate from my glamour modelling career, I want to start modelling as Jordan again.

I love the fact that I can have a career as Katie Price and a separate one as Jordan. But often when I'm promoting things under my Kate Price name, I get told not to be like Jordan and that's exactly what happened when it came to the launch of my lingerie range in December 2006. So many people have approached me to create a lingerie range with my name on it and I resisted for years. I didn't want to put my name to any old range – it had to be right for me. Plus, it's so predictable for a glamour model, or, in fact, any kind of model, to bring out their own line of underwear and I never like to be predictable. With my business head on, I also wasn't sure if there would be enough money to be made from lingerie, because there are so many different bra sizes. But then I had the idea of creating a range for women with bigger boobs. That would immediately set my lingerie apart from all the other celebrity ranges out there and make it unique to me. I'd also had lots of letters from women asking me where I bought my bras, so it looked like there was a real gap in the market for bras that were feminine and comfortable for the larger cup sizes.

I finally decided to work with a company called Panache. They're a small family-run firm and it turned out to be a good choice, as they're some of the best people I've ever worked with. They were so genuine, with no bullshit, and they were just as enthusiastic as me about the products. We agreed to make the bras from a size D through to a GG and I was really able to put my ideas into the designs. It was going to be the Katie Price range. If it had been under my Jordan name, I could probably have been more raunchy, but I wanted to keep things pretty and girlie, with plenty of pink, bows and lace – not a crotchless knicker in sight!

My lingerie was going to be sold in ASDA with a view to it going into other stores – so far so good. The one thing I didn't like was how the marketing people made such a big deal about the kind of pictures they wanted from me to promote the underwear. They kept going on and on about how I had to pose being Katie Price and definitely not Jordan. I've had a career as a glamour model and that's completely different to posing as a fashion model. A fashion model would probably stand there stiff as a board, whereas a glamour model would arch their back, and stick out their tits and that's what I'm used to doing . . . While I was posing for the pictures, the marketing people would be constantly commenting on what I was doing, criticising me and saying things like, 'No that's not right, she's pouting too much, she's looking too sexy.' They were so anal about the photographs, worrying that some of them were too much like glamour shots. I know that they're important people and they're buying my range, but, at the same time, you can't fool the public and try to erase from their heads the fact that I posed for Page 3 and that I had a career as a glamour model. Everyone knows I did! The public know that I've grown up and that I've moved on in my career. At the same time, I don't want to be the same as any other model who just stands there like a blank canvas showing off the underwear, because it's not just about the underwear, it's about me. People buy the underwear because it's my range. Of course I didn't pose provocatively, or in a way the Jordan side of me would, but I still made sure the pictures reflected me.

For the launch I was determined to do something

different. As I've already said, I love thinking of good promotional ideas and I decided I wanted to use real people wearing the underwear, not stick-thin models. I got the idea from the Dove advert, which shows all different sizes and ages of women. I thought it would be great to use my friends and family – who are a real mix of ages, shapes and sizes. ASDA loved the idea. I also thought it would be a laugh to get all my friends and family together, and that we could have a fun day getting pampered for the shoot. I was going to wear the underwear myself, too, as I think if you're going to promote something then you have to wear it, whereas other celebrities often don't when they're advertising their lingerie ranges, mentioning no names . . .

I managed to persuade ten of my friends and family, including my mum, my sister-in-law Louise and my best friend Michelle. And I know that if my nan had been alive she would definitely have wanted to take part as well! I got everyone round my house first to get measured up and so they could get to know each other. They were all quite nervous, but also excited, and everyone was saying, 'Are we mad to be doing this?' But because they were in it together and they knew they weren't typical model shapes, they egged each other on and seemed to have the attitude 'Well, if you can do it, so can I!' which was just what I wanted.

The same Jordan/Katie Price issue came up again at the launch, but I've been in this business long enough to know what pictures will get in the papers and what will sell, so I rebelled. I went for smoky-eyed, vampy make-up and big hair and I did my confident, hands-on-hips Jordan pose and, sure enough, the pictures made it into the press. At the end of the day, some people might not like the Jordan image, but it's still the name that sells. I've been interviewed and photographed for so many different magazines now, including *Vogue*, *Elle* and *Cosmopolitan*, and they all say they want to interview and photograph me as Katie Price. But on the cover it says they've got an interview with Jordan – so, as much as people want to know about the Katie Price side of me, the magazines will always use the Jordan name to promote the interview and sell copies. I guess I'm lucky that I've got two images I can use and it gives me more possibilities in my career. So I can be Katie Price for my novels and children's books, my TV shows, my lingerie and my perfume, and I can also be Jordan, the glamour model with an adult website, knowing that all the time I'm the same person. I don't wake up in the morning and think, *Oh, right, today I will mostly be Jordan!* I am very ambitious and there are so many other things I want to do. I've got ideas for clothing ranges, kids' toys, films, management . . . I even want my own production company. And who knows, perhaps one day my image will be on a stamp! I've always been ambitious, but now it's got to the point where, if I think I want to do something, I just do it! It's not about money, it's more about power and about being able to go out and do things and make a success of them.

* * *

I love working hard, but sometimes I think I get my work–life balance a bit wrong and December was no exception, because we were in the middle of promoting our album and my lingerie range while still suffering from morning sickness and moving house. The move itself was stressful – well it always is, isn't it? – and, because of our work commitments, we couldn't even have a day off. The day we actually moved, I was in Manchester doing signings to promote my lingerie range, so I left the house in Sussex in the morning and came back at night to our new house in Surrey – poor Pete had to deal with it all on his own. We had packers, but that was stressful as well, because we didn't know where anything was and for ages afterwards we just didn't have time to unpack. Pete and I had lived at my house in Maresfield, a pretty village in East Sussex, for nearly three years, and I'd spent a lot of time and money having the house done up and making it more to my taste. I had installed a hot pink kitchen – my Aga was customised and sprayed pink – and I converted my dressing room into a pink girlie paradise. I kept the décor of the rest of the house quite neutral, though, in cream and white – even I don't want pink in every room! But with two kids and one on the way, the house had become too small. Plus, in spite of all the money I had spent on it, and having the builders in what felt like all the time, it never seemed to be finished in the way I wanted – it just wasn't modern-looking enough for me.

I wanted somewhere bigger, somewhere with stables and land for my horses and, ideally, a pool. I can't stand house hunting and I don't want to look at lots of places. Usually, I know straightaway whether I like a place or not and, as soon as I saw the house in Surrey, I thought, *I love it, I want it!* It's late Edwardian – all huge windows and high ceilings – with nine bedrooms, a cottage where a housekeeper and nanny could stay, a pool, tennis court, stables and twenty-six acres of land. When I first saw the house, I thought, *Wow, this is grand!* but now I'm in it, I don't think like that – I'm used to it. To be honest, I wouldn't want a house any bigger than this. I'd never want some big, formal palace. I like smaller, cosier family houses.

I bought the house all on my own, which may be a surprise to some, because I am married and most married couples jointly own their homes. But I didn't want to have it in both our names. I said to Pete, 'You've got your houses in Cyprus and Australia and my name's not on those. I have to think of what might happen in the future.' Not that I'm imagining that we would ever split up, but I value my independence too much. And I'll never forget what happened when I broke up with one of my exes, Dane Bowers – I lost the flat we'd lived in and everything else, including my dog, to him and I ended up with nothing. Not only was I devastated by the break up, but I also had nowhere to live. I vowed then and there that I would never ever allow myself to get into that situation again. I haven't worked all my life to give my house away if my marriage broke up. I know we're married and I want to be with Pete for life, but anything could happen. He could go off and do a gig and meet a girl, fall for her and then fuck off and leave me. You just don't know. I have to think of the kids and make sure they will always have a roof over their heads.

We have a joint account for household bills and food etc, though, which we both put money into, and that is a first for me. And, of course, we have our prenuptial agreement. Pete was the one who insisted we had one that was clear about the terms. If we ever split up, I wouldn't have to give Pete anything – he would just have what was his – and nor would he have to give me anything. Having a pre-nup might not sound like the most romantic thing in the world, but I'm a realist and, because Pete was the one who wanted it, it proved yet again – not that I needed any proof – that he's with me for love, as I am with him. And although we each own houses, we are looking to buy a family house together too and I would rent out my other house.

* * *

The other big thing that happened in December was that I revealed that I was pregnant, but I hadn't even had my twelve-week scan when I decided I had to come out with the news. In the past I'd left it as long as I could get away with before admitting that I was pregnant, just because I wanted to know that the baby was okay before I told the world. When I was pregnant with Junior, for instance, I left it nearly six months before I told anyone that I was pregnant (apart from my immediate family), but it was a great pressure for me, trying to hide it and pretend to be normal. I sometimes wonder if that contributed to my Postnatal Depression. . . I think, if you're pregnant, you should be able to enjoy it (well, apart from when you're being sick) and not worry about keeping it a secret. But with this pregnancy, because I was so ill and because I'd recently had the miscarriage, I just didn't want the stress of hiding it. I wanted people to know so that, when I was interviewed, they would understand why I didn't seem quite myself and would appreciate why I felt ill. Strangely, from the moment I broke the news, my belly seemed to pop out more and I showed really early on in the pregnancy – in fact, there's no way I could have kept it a secret for long, this baby obviously wanted the world to know all about it!

By the time it came to Christmas, I was exhausted and I was really looking forward to having a couple of weeks off and chilling out with the family. I knew that 2007 was going to be a busy one – what with filming for our new reality show and going to the States to promote the first series, promoting my novel, *Crystal*, and my pony books, and not forgetting the new baby, of course! But I ended up stressing over presents. Though I have to admit that this was a nice stress to have, compared to all the others I'd had lately! The problem was what to get Pete when he already had everything he could possibly want and anything he did want he could just go out and buy himself. In the past I've bought him loads of bling and, every time I go shopping, I buy him clothes. So deciding what to get him was a nightmare! I ended up buying him a mountain bike, a golf set, a bulldog puppy, a quad bike and a remote-control car – so he did all right. I spent the few days before Christmas charging around here, there and everywhere picking up all the presents in my horse box, because they wouldn't fit in my car. And I had to collect the puppy from the breeders and settle him in the cottage so Pete wouldn't see him. Seeing how wound up I was and wondering where I had been, Pete said, 'Why are you stressing like this? I don't want to have people over for Christmas if this is what you're like.'

'I'm stressing because I've been getting all your presents!' I shot back, not exactly feeling the spirit of Christmas. And then I lost it, 'All right, if you must know, I've got you a golf set, a mountain bike, a quad bike, a remote-controlled car and a puppy. Okay? Are you happy now you know exactly what you've got?'

Of course, he was pissed off because I had ruined the surprise.

'Well,' I said, 'I'm fed up of hiding everything and having you wondering what I've been up to!'

* * *

I always buy lovely paper and want to give everyone beautifully wrapped presents, but in the end, as usual, I ran out of time and just had to wrap everything as quickly as possible, just whacking on the sellotape. When you earn good money, I always think people expect nice presents and I'd spoilt my mum and bought her a diamond watch, diamond earrings, luggage from Mulberry and some perfume and spa products. As I wrapped everything up, I thought, *How am I going to top that next year?* I don't want my family thinking I'm tight! Not that they would, I'm sure. Meanwhile, I made up with Pete following our row about presents and we both decided that next year we would have to tell each other exactly what we wanted. But even as I agreed, I thought, *Oh no, that'll ruin the surprise and I love surprises and opening loads of presents!* On Christmas Day I discovered that Pete had spoiled me as much as I had him as I unwrapped a gorgeous diamond tennis bracelet, a mountain bike, and a blind fold and handcuffs from Agent Provocateur, which I'm afraid to say have stayed in the box. I'll get them out when I've got my new boobs . . .

Christmas Day felt strange because my nan wasn't with us. My mum knew that she'd feel sad without her, so she'd booked a holiday in Australia with my stepdad and sister and they all left after Christmas lunch. Usually we'd have been together for the rest of the day and Boxing Day, eating, playing games and watching films, so Christmas didn't feel quite the same. Junior had been a bit under the weather over Christmas and he developed an extremely high temperature, so we had to take him to the emergency doctor. He was fine and just had a virus, but then, on Boxing Day, Pete also had to go to the doctor's too. All in all, I was looking forward to the New Year. We'd had to put up with so much shit in 2006. So 2007 had to be better, didn't it?

CHAPTER TWELVE

THE DAY I WILL NEVER FORGET

I was thrilled when ITV2 wanted to sign us up for a third series of our reality TV show. Pete and me have got so used to being filmed that we definitely don't put on an act for the camera – we're ourselves and we're down to earth – and I think that's what people like about us. Whereas, when you see other celebrity couples – mentioning no names, but I'm sure you know exactly who I mean – they always look immaculate and you can never imagine them arguing

– they're in their perfect little celebrity bubble. But with Pete and me, people can see that we have everything that we want, but we're still normal. We argue, we sometimes look rough – we're not perfect.

Our management team had been filming us throughout 2006 and had some great footage of all the things that had happened to us. But when we signed the new contract with ITV2, they said they didn't know where the footage would fit in. When they saw it though, they thought it was so good that they decided to use some of the footage for *The Baby Diaries*. I was a bit worried that by not using all of the existing footage, people wouldn't see us working on our album and promoting it, which had been so important to me. In fact, I was almost worried that the new series would end up being boring because not enough was happening in our lives, and that there wouldn't be enough drama in 2007. I couldn't have been more wrong . . . The start of 2007 was the stuff of any parent's nightmare. It is so deeply upsetting remembering Harvey's accident on New Year's Eve. I came close to losing my precious boy and it's something I will never, ever forget.

* * *

We decided to kick off the New Year by throwing a party for all our friends and family. I love dressing up, but didn't want to spend too much time thinking about what to wear, so I decided to have a pyjama party. I invited around seventy people and spent a couple of days getting the house ready, making sure all the guest bedrooms were furnished, buying loads of food and drink and new pyjamas for the family. I was completely organised and really looking forward to the party. On the afternoon of the party, everything seemed on track, and Pete's cousins were already at the house, along with my mum's friend Louise and her daughter Rhia, who had spent Christmas with us. Everyone was in the kitchen, getting on with the cooking and the nanny was looking after Harvey and Junior. As everything seemed to be going so smoothly, I decided that I would nip out and look at a horse I was interested in buying. People might think that New Year's Eve was a strange time, but I don't get much free time. The horse seemed great and, after I'd ridden it, I thought I would probably like to buy it. As I drove back home I was in a really good mood, thinking about the party ahead and looking forward to seeing all my friends.

As I walked inside the house, I said hi to everyone and was just taking off my wellies when I heard Harvey crying. He was upstairs and he sounded very upset, but at that stage I didn't think it would be anything serious, because he sometimes cries like this when he's frustrated with one of his toys. And so I asked the nanny if she could go and check on him. A few minutes later she shouted down to me, sounding panicky, saying that I'd better come up. *What has he gone and broken now?* I remember thinking as I walked upstairs to his bedroom. But his room was empty – this wasn't right. 'Where are you?' I called out, suddenly feeling panicky myself. She called back that she was in my bedroom and I ran there, my heart suddenly racing. It's all a bit of a blur when I try to remember what happened next, though, because I was so shocked by what I saw. Harvey was lying on my bed, crying and thrashing around in agony. As I tried to comfort him, I was frantically trying to work out how he'd hurt himself. His clothes were wet and, as I looked at his right foot, to my horror I could see blood and loose skin and I realised he must have burnt himself. But not knowing back then how to treat a burn, I quickly pulled his tracksuit trousers down and, as I did, all the skin seemed to peel away from his right leg and there was blood everywhere. Harvey was screaming, unsurprisingly, like I'd never heard him scream before. I can't tell you what it does to you to hear your child screaming in agony. I felt as if I was being ripped apart inside.

'Pete!' I shouted, 'Come up here quickly, we've got to call an ambulance.' As well as getting urgent treatment for his burn, I knew that Harvey needed his emergency cortisone injection as soon as possible, otherwise there was the danger he might go into shock; his windpipe could close up so that he wouldn't be able to breathe and he could die. I'm used to giving him a daily injection of growth hormones, but I really can't do the emergency cortisone one because the needle is so big and, in the shaken and panicky state I was in, I doubt I would have been able to do it. Pete and his brother Mike raced upstairs and I ran to call the ambulance. I had to be the one who did it because I needed to explain about Harvey's condition. I didn't know how much time we had before Harvey went into shock and I was feeling desperately anxious. Straightaway, when I dialled 999, I said, 'Please send an ambulance here, my son's had an accident – he's been burnt. And he needs an emergency cortisone injection now,' I thought I'd made myself clear, but the person on the other end said, 'Take your time, tell me your address and tell me what happened.' *I haven't got time for this!* I thought, *My son could die! Just get the ambulance here.* But summoning all my strength to be calm, I explained the situation yet again, and all the time I was struggling to contain the panic and fear inside me. The operator told me to put cold water on the burn. '*Please*,' I begged them, 'This isn't a normal burns case. My son has all these other medical problems, he really needs this injection or he could die.' But the operator didn't seem to want to know about that and instead asked me how the accident had happened, 'I don't fucking know!' I exclaimed again, 'Just please get an ambulance here.'

As soon as I ended the call, I rushed into the kitchen where Pete and Mike had carried Harvey. It was a sight I will never forget. Pete and Mike were struggling to hold Harvey and to put cold wet towels on his leg. But he was going absolutely ballistic with pain and throwing himself around the room,

screaming and crying. Harvey was covered in blood
and there was blood all over the kitchen floor. I
wanted to hold him, to comfort him, but he wouldn't
let anyone near him. We all stood there helplessly,
not knowing what to do. Finally the ambulance
arrived. I think it took twenty minutes, which is a
very long time when your child is in agony and you
think he could die. Straightaway the paramedics
wanted to get Harvey's leg under a cold shower. 'But
we've only got those walk in modern showers' I said
in despair, then realised that there was a shower you
can hold in the cottage. As the paramedics carried
Harvey there, I tried to tell them that he urgently
needed his cortisone injection. And I held out the
emergency pack for them. But they just looked at me
as if to say, 'What are you going on about?' And they
told me they had to deal with his leg first. In the
cottage, they lowered Harvey into the bath and ran
the cold shower on his leg. Harvey was still beside
himself, crying and screaming and thrashing around.
It took Pete, Mike and the other paramedic to hold
him still.

'*Please* listen to me,' I said, trying to stay calm, 'He
needs his injection now, because he's got all these

other medical problems.' I showed them his Great Ormond Street medical passport that describes his condition and what medication he needs, but the paramedics were still more concerned with treating his burn.

'Don't you understand? He will die unless he has this injection,' I shouted, on the verge of losing it. In desperation, I got on the phone to the Endocrine department at Great Ormond Street which looks after Harvey and asked them to explain about Harvey's condition to the paramedics. I could see that Harvey was going into shock – he was still trying to move, but I know my son and I know when there's something wrong. Finally the paramedics spoke to Great Ormond Street and then, thank God, they gave Harvey the injection, saying that they would have to get him to hospital immediately. While they were getting him out of the bath, I raced back into the house, knowing that I had to pack a bag with his medication, the doctor's letters explaining his condition and his nappies, because hospitals don't have the special large nappy size that he needs. Afterwards, everyone who saw me said that I seemed really calm, but all I wanted to do was make sure that

Heading off to a shoot in China.

Me and my manager Claire.

Me and my te[...]
Left to right: Nicola, Gary, [...]

In our Cyprus home.

In the pool in Cyprus. Gary and Phill, or as I like to call them, the California Twins. They are Princess's fairy godfathers.

Me and Pete try out our tennis
skills at the Cyprus house.
I won, of course.

A shoot in America.

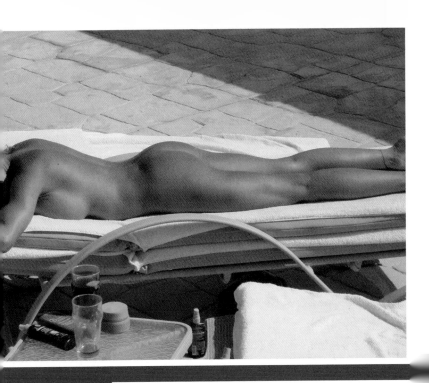

Topping up our tans.

The whole family tucks into lunch.

Harvey was all right, and I knew he needed his medication; I didn't care about anything or anyone else.

I travelled with Harvey in the ambulance and Pete followed behind in the car, as only one family member is allowed in the ambulance. It was the journey from hell. I was trying to comfort my son, but ended up having to ask the paramedic for a bowl because I was being sick from my morning sickness. As well as being desperately anxious about Harvey, I also thought, *I'm going to lose the baby because of this stress.* The paramedic was busy putting monitors on Harvey and by now he had calmed down and was no longer crying, but he didn't seem with it at all, which really frightened me. Suddenly the paramedic put an oxygen mask over his face. When I asked if he was okay, the paramedic nodded, but I thought, *No he's not.* I've watched so many real-life medical programmes on TV and this is never a good sign. The next thing I knew the paramedic was tilting Harvey's head back and asking if he has ever had any breathing problems. Struggling to stay calm, I said, 'Yes, Harvey had to have his tonsils removed because of his breathing and his windpipe can close if he suffers severe shock.' The paramedic replied that his tubes did seem to be closing and he asked the driver to pull over. For a few seconds I really thought that was it, that Harvey was going to die, because he seemed to have stopped breathing. It was the worst moment of my life. I was crying, but I tried to tell myself that Harvey would be fine, that I'd seen people come out of worse situations than this. 'I love you, Harvey,' I said, trying to blink back the tears while reaching out and holding his hand, 'You're going to be okay, I promise.' My memory of what went on at this time is very hazy because I was in such a state of panic, but the paramedic was doing something to help Harvey breathe. Then he told his colleague to carry on to the hospital and that we had to get Harvey there as soon as possible as his oxygen levels were dropping. *Please be all right, Harvey*, I kept saying over and over in my head, willing him to be okay. *Please.*

Finally we arrived at the hospital and there were at least eight doctors and nurses waiting for us. Straight-away they injected Harvey with something, took blood and put what looked like clingfilm on his leg, while I tried to explain to the doctors about Harvey's condition and about his medication. Fortunately one of the nurses recognised Harvey and me from Brighton Hospital, where she'd treated Harvey, and she said to the doctor in charge, 'Listen to the mum, she'll explain to you about his condition and his medication.' I showed the doctor Harvey's Great Ormond Street passport, and went through all the doses of medication that he was on. By now Pete had arrived, it was such a relief to have him with me, hospitals can be so overwhelming, and he was being so calm and strong for me and Harvey.

The two of us sat at Harvey's bedside. Harvey was quiet now and just lay there on his back, not saying anything, not moving. While I was so relieved that he was in hospital, it was awful seeing him in this state. His oxygen levels still weren't stable, so he was on an oxygen mask and he had heart monitors on – he looked like he was a plug socket in a wall with all these wires coming from him. It was so scary. But at that stage I had no idea just how serious Harvey's burn was. It looked awful – his leg was really pink and raw where he'd lost the layers of skin, but we didn't know how deep and severe the burn was. But, after a couple of hours, the doctors said that they couldn't look after Harvey at that hospital because of his medical condition and that he'd have to go to Chelsea and Westminster in London. I asked if he could go to Great Ormond Street instead, because the doctors there had treated him, but they explained that there wasn't a burns unit there.

I realised that I was going to have to go home and get more things for Harvey. I told Pete that I would drive back and get everything because I knew exactly what was needed and, let's face it, men are useless at knowing what to pack. Pete would go in the ambulance with Harvey to the other hospital and I would drive there. By now it was early evening and, within the next few hours, our seventy guests were due to arrive at the house. Some of them were even coming from the North, so they would already have set off. Pete and me had to text everyone, saying that Harvey had had a really serious accident and was in hospital. We said that they were still welcome to come to the house, as everything was set up for the party, but that Harvey, Pete and me wouldn't be there. I also called my mum on holiday in Australia to let her know, though at first I think I underplayed how serious the accident was, as I didn't want to worry her.

Pete walked with me to the car park. By now it was pissing it down with rain. I've never seen rain like it and I drove the car back to the hospital entrance, planning to drop Pete off and then drive home for our things. But just as I pulled up, a car reversed straight into me. I wound down my window and shouted angrily to the driver: 'You dickhead, what are you doing? Can't you fucking see?' At the same time, Pete got out and was saying, 'Mate! The car.' Then a very heavily pregnant woman got out of the passenger side, looking as if she was going to drop there and then and I could see that the poor guy was obviously panicking as his wife was in labour. 'I'm so sorry!' I exclaimed, 'Our son's just had an accident . . . I didn't realise your situation.'

Leaving Pete to sort out insurance details, I typed my home address into the Sat Nav and wearily drove home. It was a horrendous drive because the navigator directed me down narrow country lanes and the rain was so torrential I could only go at 15 mph as I couldn't see where I was going. To make matters worse, I suddenly noticed the petrol gauge was on red. *Shit!* I thought, *now I'm going to run out of petrol!* I couldn't find a petrol station anywhere and, because it was New Year's Eve, everything was shut. Fortunately I found one just in time and made it home. Some people had already turned up in their pyjamas and I repeated my offer that they should stay and enjoy the food and drink, otherwise it would all have been wasted. But they all said that they couldn't possibly enjoy themselves under the circumstances. It was so weird returning to the house. After the noise, bright lights and frenzied activity of A&E, it was so quiet and warm. Everything was set up for the party, and for a second, as I walked in, it was almost as if the hospital scenes were a terrifying nightmare . . .

I quickly packed the extra bags with clothes, nappies and toys for Harvey and clothes and wash things for Pete and me. My clothes were still covered in blood from the accident, but I didn't give a shit what I looked like. I got back in the car and this time drove to Chelsea and Westminster Hospital in London where Harvey had been transferred to the specialist burns unit. I arrived around eleven o'clock that evening. Harvey had obviously been given morphine because he was calmer. I hugged him, telling him how much I loved him, then I put some of his toys beside him, tried to make his room look more homely and sat next to him kissing his head and holding his hand. Although I was still desperately worried about Harvey, I felt reassured that he was in a safe place now, where the doctors would know how to deal with his condition and treat his burn. He was in an isolation room where the temperature was kept at a certain level to help the skin heal and there were strictly sterile conditions, because there was such a high risk that the burn could become infected. But little did I know, as Pete and me sat by Harvey's bedside, that we would be staying here for the next month and that, for a further three months, Harvey would be an inpatient needing trips to the hospital three times a week to get his burn treated.

By midnight Harvey had finally fallen asleep. Pete and me saw in the New Year by drinking cups of Appletiser with the nurses and sharing some champagne-filled chocolates. Then, later, as we lay on the spare bed in Harvey's room, Pete said, 'This is why we are so close and why we are so good as a couple, because look at all the things we've been through and look at how strong we are.' And he was right. Sometimes it's like someone is testing our relationship and emotions to see if we can last . . . As I lay in bed that night, all I could think about was poor Harvey. We worked out how he must have had his accident. Our house is completely baby-proofed – we have stair gates to prevent Harvey and Junior going upstairs on their own and upstairs we keep all the doors locked. But as we had guests staying for the party who maybe weren't as careful as us about keeping the gates shut and the doors locked, we can only imagine that someone left the gates open. It would only have taken Harvey a few minutes to find that the gates on the stairs were open. Then he must have wandered upstairs to my bathroom. I'm not saying that I blame anyone, it was an accident and it only goes to show that a few unsupervised minutes can lead to tragedy with a child like Harvey.

Before his accident, Harvey was obsessed with water, and I mean *obsessed*. Every night, just before bath time, when we were getting him and Junior ready for their bath and while we were supervising him, he liked to run the cold tap and flick the water with his hands or feel it running against his tongue. So when he discovered that my bathroom door was unlocked, he must have gone in there to play with the water, but instead of turning the cold tap on, he turned on the hot one. The taps in my bathroom only need to be moved slightly to be fully on. Once he'd turned on the tap, Harvey must have leant over the bath and tried to touch the water, but I'm guessing he couldn't quite reach and so he must have decided to get in, not realising that, by now, the water was boiling hot. And then, as the scalding water hit his right leg, he must have panicked and stood there with the water burning his leg. Somehow, even though he was in absolute agony, he must have dragged himself out of the bathroom and on to my bed. It breaks my heart to know that, for a few minutes, while he was screaming in pain, he was on his own, that no one was there for him. And, without meaning to, I had made his injury worse by pulling down his tracksuit bottoms – apparently you are supposed to leave the clothes on a burn victim because the air hitting the damaged skin hurts even more. Then you are supposed to run cold water on the burn. As Harvey was wearing thick tracksuit bottoms that must have absorbed a lot of boiling water, I instinctively wanted to get the material away from his leg, not knowing that was the wrong thing to do. A few months after his accident I took and passed a first aid course because I never want to be in a situation like that again where one of the children hurt themselves and I don't know what to do.

Because of Harvey's medical condition, this wasn't a straightforward burns case. His burn was so severe – running from the top of his thigh all the way down to his foot – that the doctors would normally have treated it by giving him a skin graft. Harvey's condition was too unstable, though, and, because of the concerns about his breathing, they were unable to give him a general anaesthetic – it really was too risky. The doctors were also worried that if Harvey had a skin graft it might not work and then he would end up with two wounds to heal.

The morning following Harvey's accident, the doctors explained that they were going to have to scrub Harvey's burn to stop the infection and to encourage the new skin to grow and that it was going to be agonising for him. I clutched Pete's hand and looked at Harvey as he slept, oblivious to what was in store for him. I couldn't bear the thought of Harvey having to suffer anymore. He woke a few minutes later and he was obviously in pain from his burn.

And what he didn't realise was that it was about to get a whole lot worse . . .

In most instances, someone who had to have this procedure on a burn would be given a general anaesthetic or so much morphine that they would be completely out of it. But Harvey couldn't have a general and, although he weighed the same as a twelve-year-old, he could only be given the morphine dose for a five-year-old, which meant the medication had little effect on him. I tried to tell Harvey that the doctors were going to help his leg get better, but I knew he didn't understand, and I was feeling more and more apprehensive about what was going to happen. An hour or so later, a group of five doctors and nurses walked into the room. They carefully lifted Harvey from the bed into a wheelchair and then wheeled him into the bathroom. I thought he would have had his own bathroom, as he was in an isolation room, but he didn't and he had to use the ward bathroom, which immediately made me worry about the risk of infection. I was by his side all the time, wanting to be brave for him, telling him that it was going to be all right. He was lifted into the bath, which freaked him out straightaway because it was full of water and, of course, thanks to his accident, his obsession with water had gone and he was extremely wary of it. They then removed the dressing and he went berserk as they touched his leg. I put my hand over my mouth in shock because I couldn't believe how terrible the burn looked now. And then they began scrubbing hard at his leg with gauze. Harvey let out a piercing scream and carried on screaming. I have never heard screams like it. He was struggling to get away from them and away from the pain. It took four people to hold him down. He was absolutely terrified and in total agony. I think I've blanked much of this time out of my mind and, when I look back, all I can remember is seeing Harvey's eyes nearly popping out of his head in horror as he looked for me, as if to say, *Help me, please! Why are you letting them do this to me, Mummy?* And yet I knew he wouldn't understand if I told him they were trying to help. All he knew was that he was being pinned down by people who were hurting him and he couldn't understand why. I had wanted to be strong for him, but I was completely overwhelmed by seeing my son in that much agony. After a few minutes, I just had to leave the room and Pete went in to be with him. I ran as far down the corridor as I could, but I could still hear Harvey screaming, even through all the fire doors. One of the nurses came and found me and led me to the ward office. I collapsed on a chair sobbing. *Why has this happened to Harvey?* I thought to myself. I don't often cry, but now I couldn't stop, because there was nothing I could do to help and I didn't want my son to be suffering so much pain. There are no words to describe how awful it was watching him go through it. It was the worst thing I have ever had to experience in my life.

Harvey had to endure fifteen minutes of his leg being scrubbed. Then it was bandaged up again and he was wheeled back into the room. 'Mummy,' he said, 'I want Mummy,' and I hugged him tight and tried to stop myself crying. I said, 'I'm here now, Harvey, it's all right.' But it wasn't all right. Every day for the next month Harvey had to endure the excruciating pain of having his injury scrubbed and every time, as he was wheeled into the bathroom, he knew what was coming next and he'd be screaming in fear, clutching on to me, looking at me as if begging me to save him from the pain. After that first time, when I'd had to leave, I summoned all my strength and stayed with him. I'd hold his hand and talk to him and I would try to distract him by holding his toys in front of him. Harvey was so brave, because he got to the point where he'd even say, 'Bath now,' as the doctors came in the room, but he never stopped screaming when they scrubbed his leg. But, as soon as they'd finished and his leg was bandaged up again, he would be calm, because he knew the pain had stopped for a while. What he was having to endure would have been terrible for anyone, but just imagine how much worse it was for Harvey, without enough pain relief, unable to understand why this was happening to him and unable to tell anyone how he was feeling. When he couldn't take anymore, he couldn't say 'Please stop!' to have a short break from the agony. No, he had fifteen minutes of the worst pain ever.

Pete and me did not leave Harvey's side during his stay in hospital. Our world shrunk to that hospital room. Harvey was all I thought about. I spoke to my mum every day to update her on Harvey and Pete was absolutely brilliant during that time, so strong for me and Harvey. I really don't know what I would have done without him. Meanwhile, Junior was in Cyprus with Pete's mum and dad, so we knew he would be well looked after and have plenty of love. Right now all our attention had to be focused on Harvey. After a few nights of sleeping at the hospital, Pete insisted that I should stay at a hotel overnight because of the risk of infection while I was pregnant. So I booked into one nearby and would go there late at night, while Pete stayed with Harvey, and return first thing in the morning. Nothing else mattered but Harvey and getting him well again. We were supposed to be filming for our new reality TV show, but my mind was on Harvey.

I told my manager 'the only time they can film is when Pete and me are going to lunch, because, apart from that, I'm not leaving Harvey's side.' And that's exactly what the production team had to do. They did understand what we were going through, though, and they didn't pressurise us to film any more than that, which Pete and me were grateful for. Because they weren't getting that much footage they wanted me to talk about Harvey's progress but I wasn't really happy about going into details about my son, it was just too personal . . .

* * *

I had to tell Dwight about the accident, of course. After I'd explained what had happened, he wanted to know how bad the burn was, asking what degree it was.

'I don't know,' I replied, 'They don't measure burns like that anymore,' and I explained how hard it was for the doctors to treat Harvey because of his medical condition. I really didn't like Dwight's attitude and felt he might somehow be blaming me for the accident. When Dwight was ready to see him, he rang to tell me.

'Okay,' I replied, not looking forward to his visit. 'I need to know exactly when you'll be coming and, I'm sorry, but you can't stay in the room for very long because Harvey really needs me with him, and I don't like to leave him.' The fact was that Harvey didn't know Dwight well enough to be left with him, especially when he was so ill and feeling so vulnerable. I know Dwight's his biological dad and entitled to see him, but this really wasn't the time for him to try and bond with Harvey. He needed me and Pete with him. And part of me wanted to tell Dwight that I didn't want him seeing Harvey, that it would confuse him too much. It was such an emotional time for all of us, and Dwight hadn't seen what Harvey had been through and was continuing to go through. *But*, I thought, *I can't argue, I'll have to let him come down*. I also needed to know when he was coming so that I could tell the hospital to expect him. We had so much press attention and I had to protect Harvey from any journalists who might try to see him. Dwight visited Harvey twice and I made sure that each time Pete and me were having lunch. I didn't want to see him myself, as I was convinced he'd have a go at me.

But I really didn't have head space to worry about Dwight because, in spite of everything, the doctors were doing, Harvey's leg wasn't healing. It became infected. It looked horrific and the smell of it was appalling. At one point it even looked like he might lose his toes. The doctors had warned me about the risk of infection, because the hospital had such a high rate of MSRI. Harvey didn't get that, but he got another infection and it destroyed all the new skin. They then used a particular kind of cream on his burn, which was supposed to help with healing, but it had the reverse effect on Harvey and destroyed all the new skin cells instead. The doctors explained that it is usually straightforward to treat a burn, but because of Harvey's condition, they really didn't know how his body would react to what they were doing. In fact, things got so bad that the doctors considered doing a skin graft after all, even though it carried so many risks.

Harvey's recovery was made even slower by the fact that he wouldn't eat anything. We couldn't get him to eat at all – he wouldn't even eat his favourite meal of chicken nuggets and chips. It was understandable, I felt, because he was in pain and who wants to eat when they feel that bad? But he became so weak and dehydrated that he had to be put on a drip, which he kept trying to pull out. He looked awful, yellow almost, and at one point they thought he had pneumonia. It was so upsetting seeing my son deteriorate in front of me. I had some pretty dark moments when I thought he was never going to get better.

The doctors had been in constant contact with Great Ormond Street, getting advice on how to treat Harvey's medical condition. All the doses of his medication had been doubled, except the growth hormones. When things got so bad that the doctors were considering doing the skin graft, my mum, who had just returned from Australia, suddenly had an idea and said, 'Why don't you double the growth hormones and see if that helps the leg heal?' At first the doctors didn't think that would make a difference, but they decided to try it anyway because they seemed to have run out of other options. After a day doubling the dose, to our huge relief, Harvey's leg finally showed signs of healing. Greg Williams, the brilliant consultant who was overseeing Harvey's treatment, actually asked if he could use Harvey as a case study, because he had never had to treat a patient with his medical condition before and this was a kind of medical breakthrough.

Once the healing process had begun, Harvey had to have physiotherapy every day to encourage him to stand on his leg. We were told that, unless he started moving it, the new skin would grow in a stiff way which would make walking extremely difficult. We had to persuade him to try to move his leg and do exercises, which he was extremely reluctant to do because it hurt so much. He was also unwilling to get out of bed because he wasn't confident in his surroundings, as he couldn't see them clearly. But the longer he stayed in bed the worse the situation became. We had to encourage him to literally take one step at a time, so one day he would maybe stand up for a few minutes longer than the day before, and so on. It really was such a slow recovery process. It took him a long time – probably three months – before he was able to walk again. The worst thing was that he had only just become confident enough to walk and run about and now it felt like he was back to square one. And while he wasn't eating, he was just getting weaker and weaker.

* * *

We decided with the doctors that it might help Harvey's recovery and encourage him to eat if we brought him back to his home environment for a few hours one day. If he felt safe, he might feel like eating. We were just organising things for Harvey's trip back when Greg Williams, the consultant, asked if he could have a word with me.

He looked serious. 'I'm afraid that you're not allowed to take Harvey out of the hospital.'

'What?' I exclaimed, looking at him in disbelief.

'I know this is absolutely ridiculous and I'm embarrassed about saying this to you, but you've been reported to Social Services.' I couldn't believe what I was hearing as Greg went on to explain that one of the doctors or nurses who had treated Harvey at the first hospital suspected us of deliberately causing Harvey's burn and had reported us.

'I know what great parents you are,' Greg continued. 'I would hold my hand up and say how good you are.' He said that he knew the kinds of parents we were, how we obviously loved our son, how we had never left Harvey's side the whole time. I hadn't realised that, in cases involving children, the doctors make a note of how often parents visit their children and what they're like around them, but it was obvious that the doctors had been monitoring us, seeing how supportive we were. He also said that he knew from the type of burn Harvey had suffered that we had not been responsible, that it had been an accident. He knew all these things, but he was not allowed to let us discharge Harvey from hospital while Social Services investigated. I couldn't believe it. I was absolutely fuming. Straightaway I wanted to speak to someone from Social Services; I wasn't going to stand for this. So Greg called up the woman in charge for me and then I spoke to her. Trying very hard to keep my cool, I said, 'You can come to my house any time you like, you can turn up unexpectedly and you will find nothing wrong. We are not the kind of parents who would do something like this to our child. Why don't you go off and do your homework about Harvey and me.' We had recently moved to Surrey, so maybe she didn't know about Harvey's condition. We'd had a whole team of people looking after him in Sussex: speech therapists, health visitors, doctors, etc, and when you move you get a different team. 'I'm in the public eye and I'm being watched all the time. Harvey sees doctors every single week and has done for the last five years and not once have they ever seen any signs of neglect. Go to his school and ask his teachers and they will say the same. Plus Pete is an ambassador for the NSPCC. I'm so upset that you think I could have hurt my son and I think it's disgusting that you are wasting time over this when there really are cases out there where children are being abused.' I can hardly remember what she said, but it was probably something about how they had to follow up the case because it had been reported and that someone from the police and from Social Services would have to come round to the house. 'You can come round,' I said, 'but if you think you're stopping me from taking my son out of the hospital, then you've got another thing coming, because this is stupid.' And the upshot was that we did take Harvey home for a few hours. Straightaway he started eating because he felt happy in his home environment, which is exactly what I thought would happen.

What hurt the most was that Pete and me work so hard to be good parents and we would never do anything to hurt our children. And, I thought, *I'm desperately worried about my son, I'm pregnant and now I've got to deal with this stress.* I was also really missing Junior, who had been away from us for two weeks. A date was arranged for Social Services and the police to come to the house and so, instead of me spending the day with Harvey, I had to waste my time with this crazy accusation. I asked Nicola from my management to be with me as a witness, as Pete was with Harvey. One police officer turned up with the head of Social Services for my area. The reason we got her was that they didn't want the story getting out because of who I am. I remember thinking, *I don't care if this gets out! I've got nothing to be ashamed of because I've done nothing wrong!* They told me that they had to follow up the case because I had been reported, but they admitted they were embarrassed about having to do it, because they had seen what we were like with the children from our TV shows and from the press.

I said, 'You can go round my whole house and check everything, but as you'll see, we are totally baby-proofed – we've got safety gates everywhere, all the sharp edges on our tables are covered up, we've got socket covers, you name it we've got it.' And I went on, 'What about all those cases of child neglect that I've read about where Social Services have been involved but they haven't stopped the child from being killed by its parents? Shouldn't you be dealing with those instead? This accusation is such an insult, because we try so hard with Harvey – ask any of the doctors who see him.'

I knew the woman from Social Services was embarrassed, but I just had to have my say. They wanted to know how I thought the accident had happened, so I took them upstairs and showed them what I thought. I guess they wanted to see if my story fitted with how Harvey's injury looked and it obviously did because that was the end of the investigation. Afterwards, everything was fine between us and Social Services. In fact, the woman in charge was really nice and has helped me with various things for Harvey since then.

I would love to know who had reported me. It must have been someone who didn't like me and who wanted to stir up press attention. But the story, or rather lack of it, never got into the press and, believe me, if it had, I would have sued their arses, as I can just imagine how some of the tabloids would have treated the story. It was such a stressful and emotional time and I really hadn't needed this on top of everything else. However, the most important thing was that Harvey was starting to make more progress and that finally we were allowed to bring him home. It was so wonderful to have him back with us, to be a family again and to see him smile, to see him get stronger, and to see him enjoy life again. He needed a lot of extra attention and love after everything that he'd been through, though, and he kept asking for 'mummy cuddles'. But he wasn't discharged from hospital for another three months. We had to take him back to the hospital three times a week to have his burn scrubbed and bandaged; then, gradually, this was reduced to twice a week; then once. He had to have regular physio on his leg as well, and that has to continue for two years after the accident. He also has to wear silicone patches on his burn and a pressure garment on his leg to keep the skin flat and protect it, as it cannot be exposed to the sun. He's only allowed out of it for an hour a day and he will have to wear it for two years. I have to massage his leg twice a day with aqueous cream to try to make the skin smooth, which he loves because the skin itches so much. His body has produced too much collagen, which is making the skin bumpy – ironic when you think of women wanting collagen pumped into their faces to make them look younger. Nearly nine months on from the accident as I write this, Harvey is able to walk and run around again, but his leg still looks awful. The new skin is so uneven and rough. The only way I can describe it is to say that it looks like crocodile skin. I can see improvement as the months go by, but sadly he will be scarred for life.

He was also emotionally affected by his accident and for a while he was terrified of having a bath. I would have to run the cold tap and let him feel that it was cold before he got in, and throughout his bath I would have to leave the cold tap running, so he would know there was nothing to be afraid of. He had been such a good swimmer, and I was really worried that he wouldn't want to do it anymore, but fortunately by the summer he wanted to get back in the water. It helped that the water was cool, as it didn't frighten him. Poor Harvey, I can't believe how much he has been through and yet, throughout it all, he has been so incredibly brave.

CHAPTER THIRTEEN

STATESIDE

At the beginning of April 2007 we flew out to LA to promote the first two series of our reality TV show, which had been bought by E! Entertainment. It took two years and many, many meetings to arrange the deal. Even before that, though, there had been interest in me from various TV people there. During those two years, while everyone around me was getting excited about the deal, I stayed cool, not believing it would actually happen until the contracts were signed. I kept thinking, *Pete and me on American TV? No chance.* We had a really positive first meeting with the people from E! and they were saying 'It's going to be so great to have your series!' and giving us all the chat and the charm. And so I agreed, but inside I thought, *Whatever!* because I've had so many people in the past saying that this deal or that deal will be fantastic and then fuck all happens. But, in this instance, two years on we had the deal. It was really going to happen and finally I could allow myself to be excited. E! broadcasts to 600 million homes and our series was going to be on every day. I know that 600 million Americans weren't going to be watching it – they have so many channels over there – but I was still pleased. And E! is a channel Pete and me enjoy watching at home – they broadcast *The Simple Life* and also *The Girls Next Door*, which is all about Hugh Hefner's Playboy bunnies – so I thought it was the perfect place for our show.

E! loved the fact that we were British and different and Pete and me were really looking forward to flying to the States to promote our show. We were booked to do ten days of full-on interviews and shoots and then our series would air the following week. We were promoting the series right in the middle of filming the third series of our ITV2 show, *Katie and Peter: The Next Chapter*, which seemed like perfect timing to me. But apparently one of the TV executives said they didn't even want to film our America trip, as they thought it would be a waste of time. Luckily our management team said they would pay for the crew to follow us, and it was just as well they did, because we got a fantastic response.

I was really looking forward to the trip. Harvey was so much better – his leg was healing and he was back to walking confidently again. A couple of really positive things had happened to me and the family as well. Firstly, I was voted Celebrity Mum of the Year – it was great to know that people realised how important my children are to me, and how seriously I take being a mother. But although it was an honour, I didn't feel that I had to have an award to show that I'm a good mum. Still, it was good to win it, especially after the false accusation that I'd been responsible for Harvey's accident, and it was also only a few years ago that some newspapers were printing stories saying that I was the mother from hell. Secondly, the whole family, including my mum, had got to meet the Queen at the opening of the Richard Desmond Children's Eye Centre, part of the Moorfields Eye Hospital. This had been one of the charities we supported with our album and it was also special to us because Harvey had been going to Moorfields since he was a baby. So meeting the Queen really meant something to us. I remember her walking up the stairs and, as I've already said, I'm not normally phased by anyone, but she had such an aura about her. I was also impressed that she seemed genuinely interested in Harvey. I had taught Harvey to say 'Hello your Majesty' and I was really proud when he said it at the right moment.

By April, I felt for the first time in months that I could enjoy myself. I felt better than I had in ages, as I was past having morning sickness and I was in the blooming stage of pregnancy, even though I felt I looked like Big Bird! So I wanted to look as good as I possibly could for the trip to LA. By now I was seven months pregnant with a full-on bump, so my options were slightly limited. Though, you know me, I like to push it. So the week before we were due to fly out, our stylist, Kerrie-Ann, came shopping with me in London to help choose some outfits. Normally

I love buying clothes, but that day whatever I tried on made me feel fat, frumpy and ugly – it didn't matter how many times Kerrie-Ann told me I looked good and that I was pregnant, not fat, as that's just how I felt. And I thought, *It's so typical that yet again, when I've got something really big on in my career, I'm pregnant!* I felt especially insecure because you always have this idea that LA is full of beautiful women – all blonde hair, big boobs, stick-thin bodies, looking immaculate – even though I know it's not really like that at all, it's got just as many mingers as anywhere else!

We went to Zara and Selfridges for my clothes. I wanted to get some really brightly coloured outfits – in pinks, yellows, turquoises – because I love wearing those colours and I've never been one for wearing black. I'll occasionally wear a black dress, but only occasionally. We also got Pete some clothes – shirts and T-shirts mainly – as we like to co-ordinate our outfits. As we shopped I was almost as excited about buying my new clothes as going to the States, because *I love to shop* and don't get the chance to go as often as I'd like, what with my work commitments and the family.

As I was getting too pregnant to traipse around London, I'd hired Rob, the guy who usually drives us for work, to drive us round to the different shops. I thought that I'd disguised myself by not wearing any make-up, but I got noticed in the shops anyway and that was a bit of a hassle, because I was a woman with a mission – I needed to get those outfits! That weekend, Pete's parents were staying with us and Pete had said earlier that he was going to take them and Harvey and Junior to a farm for a day. It was a nice thought, but I knew it wasn't a good idea because of how hard Harvey finds it to handle new environments, especially if I'm not there. I had already booked this shopping trip with Kerrie-Anne before I knew Pete's parents were coming over, though, and it was basically a work day, as I was paying her as my stylist. Sure enough, when Pete called halfway through the day, he was in a state, 'Oh my God! Harvey will not stop crying. What shall I do?' He'd had to leave the farm and come home because Harvey had got so upset. 'Just let him calm down in his room,' I told Pete. When Harvey gets in that kind of state you have to be very calm and firm, which does require a lot of patience. But I knew that if Harvey was just given some space he would calm down in his own time. Lately I've realised that men stress far more about children crying. I'm much more laid back about it when one of the kids kicks off than Pete is. After the call, I had to rush the shopping trip, choosing outfits as quickly as we could, as I knew I had to get home for Harvey.

That day, Pete was being filmed for the TV series, which probably made it more stressful for him, but when I saw the episode I thought Pete handled both the kids really well. He was worried that he came across as being too strict with them, but I thought he was great. He was patient, calm and, although he was getting stressed, he didn't lose his temper. He's such a good dad.

I was so pleased with my purchases for the trip. I had my matching bags, shoes, necklaces and earrings and I was so excited about wearing my new things you'd have thought I was a little kid. There was only one slight problem – in the week between me buying the clothes and our trip, I had grown even bigger and some of the clothes didn't fit me anymore – luckily, I'd bought so many things that I wasn't going to be short of an outfit. And everything else was organised

– all the childcare arrangements were in place for the boys and I knew they were going to be well looked after. I didn't even have to do my packing, because Kerrie-Ann did it for me – all I had to do was pack my toiletry bag. So everything was cool and we were ready for the States. Except, typically for us, we had one moment of panic the night before when Pete couldn't find his passport, but luckily Claire, our manager, had it.

The next day we arrived at the airport in plenty of time, a first for us, as we're usually late. I didn't know whether there'd be any press at the Heathrow end, but I thought I'd better not dress in my trackies in case they were there and I wanted to look half decent. So I'd squeezed myself into my size 6 skinny jeans – obviously I couldn't do up the zip, so I held them together at the top with a hair band and wore a long mint-green top, accessorising with matching sunglasses. And thank God I had made the effort, because there were loads of paps waiting for us. There were so many of us to check in: Claire, Kerrie-Ann, the ITV film crew – Roy and Emma – me and Pete, plus the film equipment. It took us nearly an hour and a half, in the end. And, all the time we were waiting, the paps were taking picture after picture of me and Pete. I thought, *Bloody hell! That's a lot of shots of us doing absolutely nothing. Just how many do they want?* Still, it was all good publicity for the trip and for the new series, so I wasn't complaining.

After we'd checked in, we had breakfast in the VIP lounge, where we saw Russell Brand and got chatting to him. He was on the same flight as us as he was off to Hawaii to star in a film. I think he's a great character and he is exactly the same in real life as he is on TV – cheeky and funny. As soon as I got on the plane, I did what I always do and I asked for a pair of pyjamas, an extra pillow and a duvet, because I always get so cold on the flight. And then it was off with the heels and the jeans and into my cotton pjs. I then tied my hair back into a ponytail, took off all my jewellery and make-up and wrapped myself up in the duvet. I was feeling excited, though I really didn't know what to expect, and I thought this would be make or break time for our Stateside career. Flying is one of the few chances I get to relax, so I sat back to eat and sleep. Though I did watch a documentary about anorexic girls in the States during the flight, which was depressing, but I'm fascinated by those kinds of real-life stories.

Before we landed I changed back into my jeans, top and heels, let my hair down, and put on lip gloss and sunglasses so that I was prepared just in case any paparazzi were at the airport. We also decided to split up into smaller groups as we thought airport security staff would ask us too many questions if we went through together. I was the last one to go through. I was expecting it to take a matter of minutes, instead I was told there was a problem with my passport and I was escorted to a side room while they checked it out. I walked in to discover Russell Brand sitting there – they needed to check something about his passport as well. So we both sat there chatting – about what he'd been up to, about his girlfriend, about me and Pete – and we said we'd try to meet up for dinner. It turned out airport security thought I had two passports, which set alarm bells ringing. (I had lost my passport when we moved house in December and had gone to the London passport office to get a new one.) I do get annoyed whenever I go there, because it always seems like everyone is so interested in getting autographs from Pete and me that they don't concentrate on the admin. In this instance, they hadn't documented that I'd lost a passport, which is why the US authorities thought I had two. It took several hours to sort the problem out and, even though it was great chatting to Russell, I was starting to get pissed off. *I hope this isn't a bad omen for the rest of the trip,* I thought to myself.

Eventually someone from airport security came in and said, 'Are you the pregnant Jordan?' I thought, *Isn't it bloody obvious that I'm pregnant! My bump was poking out of my tight top.* Though I was surprised that she knew who I was. 'There are lots of paparrazi outside,' she went on. I wasn't expecting that kind of welcome, so I said to Russell, 'I bet they're waiting for you,' *And your ball bags!* I thought cheekily. But the problem with Russell's passport was cleared up and he was able to leave before me. Left on my own, I felt like a right criminal, especially when I said I needed a wee and I was taken to the toilet by a police officer! Eventually, though, the problem was sorted out and I was allowed to go.

'Oh my God! Pete!' I exclaimed, as we walked through Arrivals and were confronted by a wall of photographers with their cameras and video cameras focused on us. They were all calling out our names or variations on our names – for some reason they shouted out Kelly as well as Katie, or maybe it was just their accents – as they clicked away. I just wasn't expecting such a turnout from the press. I thought there'd probably be a couple of photographers, but nothing like this. It was manic! There were probably fifty paps surrounding us. I'd never had a response like it abroad – when I'd arrived in China it was full-on with the press, but nothing like America, and America was the place where I wanted the attention.

In contrast to the paps in this country, where they have a dog eat dog mentality and are often rude and don't give a shit if they get in each other's way, in LA they were really polite. They gave us space and didn't crowd us, and it seemed like they were working together to get their pictures. As we got into our car to be driven to the house we'd rented in Beverly Hills 90210, which is one of *the* places to stay in LA, we were followed by at least six huge 4x4s full of press and it gave me such a buzz. *I can't believe they're here for little us!* I thought. But I couldn't resist being cheeky and, when Pete said in amazement, 'Wow, there's so much press!' I answered, 'Pete, they're only here for me!' But I was just teasing him, because I was as excited as he was. It is so hard to break America – just to have had one pap taking pictures would have been brilliant, never mind a whole pack.

The photographers followed us all the way to our house. I thought that they'd wait on the road, but they drove right up to the front door. I'd have been outraged if this had happened in England, because I would have been protective of the children and our privacy. And if we get followed by the paps in England, we always wonder what their game plan is and what story they're trying to spin. But, here, we didn't mind, even though we realised it meant that, from then on, they would be following our every move. There are so many people who try to break America and to have all these paps staking us out showed that we were on our way . . .

We had a packed schedule of TV and magazine interviews – including the showbiz programme *Extras*, *People* magazine and *OK!* America. And they all seemed to go really well. The Americans we met were so charming and nice, but I think you have to be wary of that sometimes, and you can't always believe what people say. One of the presenters knew Pete and had been one of the dancers in his music videos. And it was funny because, before the interview, I had said to Pete that she looked like his type, and he'd made some comment about how she might have been back then but that she wasn't anymore. And then during the interview she told Pete that she'd met him before. My stomach lurched, *If he's shagged her, there'll be trouble* . . . But he couldn't even remember meeting her. It was only when they played the music video and she showed Pete a picture of the two of them that he did. After the interview he told me that he didn't think he'd shagged her, but, to be honest, I reckon anything is possible with him.

We met up with the executives from E! and they were really enthusiastic about the show. I think they liked us because we're so down to earth and normal and our shows aren't scripted at all, which is quite unusual for a reality TV show involving celebs. Other celebs just don't allow the kind of access that Pete and me do. But I'm happy to be filmed. I've been in front of the cameras since I was seventeen, and, even before I met Pete, I filmed two documentaries. Other people have video cameras to film parts of their life and we're the same, except that we have a camera crew filming us and it's all professionally done! While we were in LA, our series was being heavily trailed on TV and in the press. We were being promoted as the UK version of *The Newlyweds*. If people didn't know who we were now, hopefully they soon would! I am a big fan of *The Newlyweds'* stars Jessica Simpson and Nick Lachey. I think Jessica's stunning and they seemed like a really good couple, but she got more famous than him and then they broke up. I don't know if the reality show led to the break up, but I hope it doesn't happen to me and Pete, although our marriage has lasted longer than theirs.

The American networks liked interviewing us when we were out and about doing something, rather than just sitting in the studio, which is what I'm used to with the TV interviews I do in this country. I don't get nervous for TV interviews anymore, but I was surprised by how long the interviews took. *Jesus Christ,* I'd be thinking, *How many more takes do they want us to do! I'm in heels, I'm pregnant – get on with it!* But then I'd think this is what we're here for, so just smile and go along with it. So, for example, we were interviewed at the famous Pink's hot dog stand

and we were interviewed in the Beverly Center — a huge indoor shopping mall, a real shopaholics paradise, with practically every designer shop you could think of. Because we had so many different interviews, we changed outfits at least three times a day. Kerrie-Ann sorted out all our clothes. In fact, when I walked into my dressing room, it was exactly like walking into a clothes shop, as she had arranged all my clothes, shoes and accessories in order and I loved it! And all the time when we were out and about, the paps were following us and photographing our every move, which we didn't mind, though it was a bit full on. We're used to having our pictures taken over here, but we'd never experienced anything like America. It was a good vibe, though, and at times it was surreal. We went into the Kitson boutique on one side of the road and then decided we wanted to go to the Kitson kids' shop on the opposite side and, as we crossed the road, we were followed by at least thirty paps, which must have looked so bizarre to the drivers waiting at the crossing. Another time we went into a shop selling beauty products and Claire asked the photographers if they would mind giving me five minutes to do some personal shopping — the shop front was absolutely covered in cameras and it was just mad! The police were even called because pedestrians couldn't get past the photographers. The paps did stop photographing me as requested, though. I can guarantee that would never happen in England – even if you begged the paps, they'd carry on snapping away and be evil with it. In LA, because the paps were so nice, we'd be friendly back and we'd chat to each other.

Although our trip was packed with interviews, we did manage to fit in some fun things for ourselves. I went along to see a clairvoyant – I'm very cynical about their readings but I'm also interested in what they've got to say. I walked into her store while I was being pursued by paps, so I thought that she would know straightaway that I was famous and that that would affect her reading. I thought that, if she talked about what good things I had coming up in my career, I would just think that's bullshit as she could see the press. However, I did get very emotional when she asked me to tell her what one of my wishes would be and I found myself almost in tears as I talked about Harvey and how I wished he could see and didn't have his medical condition. I don't know why I had that reaction, because I'm so used to looking after him now. Maybe it was because I was pregnant and my hormones were making me extra emotional . . . She said various things that I took with a pinch of salt, though I was intrigued when she said I was having a girl! But then I realised she had a 50 per cent chance of getting it right!

I also went and saw a surgeon about having another boob job. I chose him because I'd been impressed with his work on the TV show *Extreme Makeovers* and, when I had emailed Hugh Hefner to ask him who he would recommend for me, he suggested the same surgeon. When I saw the surgeon, he told me that I would have to wait for six months after I'd had the baby before I could have the op. You only have to wait three months in England, so I was a bit frustrated! But then I thought, *For once, do things properly and take the advice!* So I booked myself in for December. Meanwhile, Pete did something so sweet for me – he got my name tattooed on his wedding ring finger. I loved the fact he'd had it done there, because, if he goes out without his wedding ring, he's still showing my name, showing that he belongs to me! So he must love me, as I don't know many other men who would do that for their wives.

At night we'd go out to dinner at some of the most exclusive restaurants in LA, including The Ivy and Mr Chows. Mr Chows gave us the meal on the house (apparently it's very expensive) and allowed us to film inside the restaurant, and usually they never allow filming. Paris Hilton invited us to one of her house parties too, but I didn't get the text until late one evening and, because I was pregnant, I didn't think I was up to going. I needed to sleep, as we were in LA to work, not to party. We were there ten days and it was work, work, work from the moment we got up – what with interviews, magazine shoots and filming. We had expected it to be busy and it was, but we enjoyed it – we wanted the exposure, we wanted our series to do well. Wherever we went we had a good response, as everyone seemed really excited to see us and we were already getting recognised by people in the street as they'd seen the show being trailed. They'd come up to me and Pete and say, 'Hi, I can't wait to watch your show!' We were both really pleased that we were making an impact.

Of course we weren't the only British celebrities out in LA – Victoria Beckham was also out there as well. I was asked about Posh and Becks in a couple of interviews and, back in the UK, it was made out to be a far bigger thing than it actually was. We were asked if we knew who they were and what she did. How could I not know who she was! I was perfectly polite and replied, 'He's a footballer and she used to be in a girl band, but now she's a footballer's wife.' I wasn't being bitchy, I've got past that stage and I don't know what she does. The press always made out that there was this feud between us but there wasn't really. Yes, it upset me when she sang 'Who Let the Dogs Out?' obviously aimed at me all those years ago at Old Trafford, and, yes, I didn't like the way she was around Dane Bowers when I was going out with him and the two of them were recording their single – I felt she tried to exclude me and line Dane up for one of her mates – but that's water under the bridge now, as I'm happily married and in a completely different place. It's history. I heard that she wanted to make up and go out for dinner, as we're both British and we're both in the States. I thought even if that was true, and I'm not sure if it was, I don't give a shit about her. The fact that we're two Brits in LA isn't a good enough reason for me to go out for dinner. If she didn't want to know me at home in the UK, why does she want to know me out in the States? But if it was in England and she asked me to go out for dinner, and it wasn't in front of any press, I wouldn't turn her down. And I would invite her and David to our house so our kids could play, but I doubt she'd accept the offer.

As soon as the British press picked up on the fact that I'd been asked about Victoria they ran stories with headlines like 'Jordan has a dig at Posh' and 'Posh Vs Jordan', 'Rivals set for Stateside Scrap'. It was all bollocks! I heard that she wanted the show she was recording about her move to the States to be scripted and yet, when her programme came out in the summer, I didn't think she did herself any favours and didn't come across well at all – I thought she seemed unapproachable, not very down to earth and far too worried about what people think, which was a shame, because I wanted to like her. She always looks the bollocks, but if she actually had no make-up on for once and was dressed casually, people might be able to relate to her. Everything was too staged and scripted. It did seem like she was taking the piss out of herself, but I wondered if she really was. For example, the scene where she had to get her

We met Prince Charles at the
Royal Variety Performance and
I was particularly excited to be
next to Take That as we waited.

We presented an award at the World Music
Awards and I met Paris Hilton too.
We have been friends ever since.

The Pricey gets to work (not airbrushed, ha ha).

My younger sister Sophie is just like me.
I had so much fun doing this shoot with her.

Top: Launching my lingerie range. I'm always boosted by the interest the press show in me and Pete.

Left: I love coming up with fun ideas for publicity stunts. For the launch of my novel, *Crystal*, I was carried in a crystal carriage.

I didn't let my baby bump get in the way.

Shooting the video for our first single together.

driver's licence photo done and she wanted it air brushed. If it was me, I'd just go to the photo booth in ASDA to get my photo done, because who gives a shit! Anyway, we've already got our foot in the door in the States, so we don't need to be pictured with any celebrities to get publicity – we can get our own. I said to Pete, 'Do you realise that we're in America and we've got a series and we haven't got it by hanging out with anyone famous, we've done it all ourselves.' And I think that's so much more of an achievement than going to all those parties to be photographed with whoever happens to be flavour of the month. We don't need anyone to help us make it, we're ourselves and we want to be accepted as ourselves and not just for who we know. At the end of the day, good luck to the Beckhams; they live in a different world to us. They're obviously the favourites in the press, whereas, whatever Pete and me do, we get slated or the story is angled so that we come out as the chavvier couple. But that's cool by us, because, at the end of the day, we've got our pay cheques and we're laughing all the way to the bank. And whatever the press over here would have you believe, when we were in LA, a lot of people we met didn't seem interested in Posh and Becks. They're not as big out there as you'd think they would be. My Posh comment was blown out of all proportion in England, of course, and yet in America they weren't bothered about it at all.

On our last day we had some time off, so we spent the morning at Universal Studios in Hollywood. There were some amazing rides in the theme park and usually I'm a total daredevil and love going on them – the scarier the better – but I couldn't when I was so heavily pregnant. And that day I could hardly bear to watch the rides because I felt really sick. I didn't know whether it was morning sickness again or whether I had a bug, but I felt crap. We then went on the studio tour – a behind-the-scenes look at how movies are made. But as we travelled around the film sets in a little buggy, I threw up everywhere. We were being filmed by our ITV crew for our series and, as usual, the paps were following us. *Please don't let them get a shot of me puking!* I thought. However, by the afternoon I was feeling better and now it was Pete who was complaining that he felt unwell. We had been invited to Hugh Hefner's mansion that night for dinner and to watch a movie with him. I'd met Hef several times before – most memorably in 2002 when I posed nude for *American Playboy* – and I was looking forward to catching up with him, because he's such a character, a real charmer and a really nice man. But because Pete was ill and I didn't want to go on my own, I cancelled. Besides, as much as I had enjoyed the trip, it had knackered me out. So, in the afternoon, Pete stayed in bed and I went shopping at The Grove – another fantastic shopping area in LA. It would be my last chance to shop for a while, so I had to make the most of it. On the way back we picked up a KFC but when I returned to our room, Pete was still saying he felt ill and was lying in bed. Although I was sympathetic, I wasn't too worried; I thought he just had a stomach bug and he'd be fine the next day and that he'd get over it. I always think men exaggerate how ill they are. But, in this instance, I couldn't have been more wrong.

CHAPTER FOURTEEN

PLEASE GET BETTER

The next day Pete woke up saying he felt even worse, that he had a pounding headache and felt nauseous. In the VIP lounge, as we waited to board our flight, we were given a complimentary bottle of champagne – poor Pete, alcohol was probably the last thing he felt like being near. Gary opened the bottle and the cork flew into the air and narrowly missed hitting a little girl. When we looked over, we saw the film star Matt Damon with her. 'Sorry!' we exclaimed. And even though Pete felt so rough, he said to me, 'Don't look at him, Kate!' He knows that I used to think that Matt was fit. It turned out that he was on the same flight as us and was sitting really near me. And even though Pete still felt ill and kept disappearing to the bathroom to be sick, every now and then he'd tell me not to look at Matt. 'I'm not, Pete!' I said, and it was true – I was talking to my manager and reading a magazine. Matt's a good-looking man, but he was there with his wife, baby and little girl and I was heavily pregnant, so it wasn't as if I was going to wink and flirt with him. And, anyway, as if he'd be looking at me, even if I wasn't pregnant!

Pete slept in the car all the way home. We were both really looking forward to seeing the boys but, because Pete didn't want to give them his bug, he didn't want to get too close to them. Poor Junior was almost beside himself, as he's such a daddy's boy and he's too little to understand why Pete couldn't hug him. It was really heartbreaking seeing him run up to Pete only for Pete to say that he couldn't pick him up. I gave him lots of cuddles to make up for it and kept him entertained, but I knew he wanted his dad as well. Pete could only manage to stay downstairs for a few minutes, though, before he had to go to bed.

We had arrived back on Sunday and were due to start filming for our TV series again on Tuesday. It was going to be a full-on week. The third series of our show had just started on ITV2 and the pressure was on to film us. I couldn't help thinking that the tight schedule was a bit unfair on Pete and me. The production team knew we'd had such a busy time in the States and we needed time to rest, especially since I was pregnant, and now Pete was ill too. On Monday Pete was still being sick and he was too weak to get up. I was so concerned about him that I ended up calling the doctor out. He checked Pete over and prescribed him antibiotics but he also had something to say to me, 'You look exhausted. I'm signing you off work for five days. You're heavily pregnant, you need to rest.' It was true, I did feel knackered and run down and I obviously looked as bad as I felt, because I hadn't even needed to mention it to the doctor.

And so the filming had to be put back. That week was so stressful. Pete just wasn't getting any better; in fact, he seemed to be going downhill. I was seriously worried about him. He wasn't eating anything and every time he had a drink he was sick and he kept saying his head was killing him. I ended up calling the doctor out three times because Pete was so poorly. By Saturday morning his condition had deteriorated so much that I called the doctor again, and this time, when I explained how Pete was, he told me to call an ambulance immediately. I couldn't believe that we were back in this nightmare situation again with someone in the family being seriously ill. It had barely been four months since Harvey's accident and now here I was dialling 999 again . . .

As soon as Pete was admitted to hospital he was put on a drip – he must have been so dehydrated from not drinking anything for over five days – but he was still being sick. He still seemed really ill, yet the following morning he was discharged. I drove him home and, as we drew near to our gates, we saw paparazzi waiting outside and Pete said he was going to throw up. 'Hold on till we get through the gate!' I told him. The last thing I wanted was for the paps to get a shot of that. So, as soon as I'd parked by the house, well away from any camera lenses, he got out of the car and threw up, and then he said, 'Oh my God, I've got to go to bed.' And he carried on being sick. 'They never should have let you come out of hospital,' I told him anxiously, 'No way are you well enough.' So I called the hospital and they told me to bring him straight back in. So much for discharging him.

Pete was in hospital for nearly two weeks. I was desperately worried about him. The doctors didn't know at first what was wrong with him and Pete was getting weaker and weaker and more out of it every time I saw him. One night I was with him and his temperature soared from 38.6°C to 39.7°C within forty-five minutes. It was so frightening, but, when I asked the doctors what they were doing to help him, they kept saying, 'We're doing the best we can.'

I just couldn't understand why they didn't know what was wrong with Pete. On one of her visits to the hospital to see Pete, my mum ended up having a go at the registrar, saying, 'He's been in here a week and you still don't know what's wrong with him. What's going on?' And all he could say was that Pete had a bug and that they didn't know what kind. It made me so scared for him, because if they didn't know what was wrong with him, how did they know how to treat him?

To make matters worse, he was stuck in some

horrible, dirty, side room in A&E with no window, no facilities, no phone and no TV. And ill as he was, people were still asking him for his autograph, which really annoyed me because no way was Pete in any fit state to be hassled like that. We tried to get him into a private hospital, but they wouldn't take him because the doctors couldn't say what was wrong with him.

As well as feeling almost beside myself with worry for Pete, I felt under such pressure. I'd had five days off from filming for our TV series, but I was now being filmed again and, because Pete was so ill, all the focus was on me.

Our last two TV series included quite a bit of footage of our old house, but when we moved into the new house in Surrey, I realised that I had to have some privacy. During the first half of 2007 I felt as though none of my life was private and it was really starting to get to me. Yes, we had signed up to do the TV series and, yes, I wanted it to show the real us, but, at the end of the day, I really needed some space and some privacy just for me and my family. I felt that if the producer really wanted to film us in a house, in every room, then they should hire one for us to live in, because I don't want burglars watching the series to see our possessions. The kidnap threat taught me to be a lot more cautious and protective of my family.

In fact, the filming for this third series had been such a different experience compared to the first two series. Before, it was just Shauna or Nicola from our management team, who we knew really well, following us around with the camera and it was always fun and relaxed. Roy and Emma, who filmed us for the third series, are really nice and I've no problem with them, it was just that the filming was much more full on. I suppose that was to do with the fact that there was such a tight turnaround between them getting the footage, editing it and then it being broadcast in April. And the shows looked great, so I can't complain. But the constant filming got to me, especially when such upsetting and stressful things had happened, what with Harvey's accident and Pete's illness. I ended up saying to my manager, Claire, 'Being filmed from Monday to Friday, from early in the morning to the evening is completely unnecessary. I know they aren't going to use all that footage. Why can't they say what they want to film, get it done in three or four hours and then everyone can go home? It's too much.' What was draining me was that I was being microphoned up from the moment I got up in the morning to the evening when I drove to the hospital to see Pete. And because Roy and Emma were in the car with me, interviewing me, it meant I had absolutely no time to switch off and unwind. When I'm in the car I want to be able to call one of my friends up or listen to music, but I couldn't during this time. Then it was straight into hospital to see Pete – a sixty-mile round trip – and I would stay there until midnight. By then it would be too late for me to call one of my friends, so all I was doing was driving home, having a bath, going to bed, getting up, being filmed, and then going to the hospital all over again. I was exhausted and stressed. At the same time, I was trying to look after the boys and spend as much time as I could with them, run the house, and do the shopping and washing. I couldn't expect our nanny to work longer hours. I know lots of people have to deal with stressful times when their partners are ill, but it was made so much tougher because I was so heavily pregnant. My mum takes Harvey to school, so she couldn't help any more than she was. She's the only person who can do the school run and I didn't want him to miss school while she stayed and helped me.

Eventually the penny seemed to drop with the production team that there was no point filming hours and hours of footage, and, while Pete was in hospital, they decided only to film what was worth filming, but it had taken them nearly the whole series to realise that! I am so much happier if we work like this, the filming's fun again. I don't want to be filmed non-stop, as it's just not humane, in my opinion, and I end up moaning – anyone would, believe me. Even though I'm used to the cameras by now, I'm still aware that I'm being filmed. Also Pete and me are pretty laid back about what they can film and what goes into the programmes. It's not like I'm demanding editorial control or I'm really precious about how they film me – I'm filmed with no make-up on or no hair extensions in and in my tracksuit, unlike other celebrities . . . However, there were a couple of things I would rather they had cut. For instance, I didn't like the footage of me at Furniture Village when I was ordering sofas for the new house. 'I don't want the prices of the things I'm buying left in,' I told Claire,

'You can see what store I'm in and people know how much things cost there, and it isn't that expensive, so please let me have some privacy. People don't need to know exactly how much I spent.' But Claire said that they couldn't edit the film because it was too late and that did piss me off, as it was something so small that I was asking to be changed. When I carried on complaining, Claire added, 'Look, it's funny, because one minute in the episode you're talking about buying a four-hundred-grand car and then the next you're quibbling about the price of cushions.' I could see her point and I said, 'Fine, keep in what I said at the store, but tell the production team to blur out the prices of the sofa.' But, when I watched the programme, I saw that they hadn't.

* * *

When I was with Pete, I did my best to try and cheer him up – I took in pictures of the kids and every day I'd take him a freshly washed towel, so he could smell home. I also bought him food (not that he felt like eating until towards the end of his stay in hospital) and I tried to make his room as comfortable as possible. But it was so upsetting seeing him lying in the hospital bed, a shadow of himself. He was so disoriented and weak because he hadn't eaten for so long. On the night his temperature rocketed, the doctors needed to change the position of his drip because his arm was so sore. However, they had real difficulty finding a vein to get the new drip in – when your temperature gets that high your veins shut down, I suppose as a way of protecting your body. Three doctors tried to find a vein in his arms, hands and feet but with no success, and Pete, understandably, was getting more and more distressed. 'Come on!' I said, 'Can't you get someone in who knows how to do it; you can see how upset he is.' So another doctor, who I hadn't met before, came in a few minutes later. He tilted Pete's bed back, which was agony for Pete, as he still had such a pounding headache and the blood rushing to his head made it worse. Then he told Pete he was going to put a line into his neck and he was tapping away trying to find a vein. By now Pete was really distressed because he was in agony. It was so awful seeing him suffer like that. I sat next to him, squeezing his hand, trying to reassure him, even though I'm needle phobic and watching the doctor trying to get the needle in was making me feel ill. Pete was crying out in pain and even though the doctor was still confident that he could get the drip in, in the end he couldn't, so Pete had gone through all this for nothing. Eventually the doctor called the anaesthetist, who got the needle in first time, and I thought, *Why didn't they do that in the first place?* It really pissed me off, because Pete was so ill – he's not some guinea pig to be practised on. I've seen this happen so many times before with Harvey, and it's awful to watch someone you love go through that much pain.

Pete was given a brain scan and the hospital didn't even manage to inform me that they were doing it, which also pissed me off, because I would like to have been there with him. Luckily his brother Mike was with him, but I wished it had been me. I'm his wife, he needed *me*. Then, the day before the hospital finally discovered what was wrong with him, I called Pete to ask if he wanted me to bring anything in for him and he was really, really down. 'What's the matter?' I asked, immediately worried, as it wasn't like Pete to sound like this. 'I've just had the most agonising experience of my life, and I really wanted to cry,' he said. 'The doctors stuck a needle into my back and it fucking hurt!' He was talking about the lumbar puncture he'd had, to see whether his spinal fluid was infected. If it was, it would mean he had Viral Meningitis. Apparently it is one of the most painful procedures you can have done. But this hadn't been explained to Pete, or, if it was, he was too out of it to take it in, so he didn't know what the hell was happening to him and he had no one with him. I hated to think of him going through this without me by his side.

Desperately worried as I was about Pete, I also felt as if I was sinking under the stress. I was eight months pregnant and I was being filmed, looking after Harvey and Junior, running the house and visiting Pete. I was hardly getting any sleep. I had to put on an act in front of the cameras that I was fine when I wasn't. And I felt like I'd let myself go because I had no time to look after myself. I looked run down – I hadn't got my hair extensions in because I'd had no time to have them done and I never feel myself without them. And all I wanted to do was to be with Pete, I didn't care about anything else. But, because of the filming schedule, I just wasn't given the time. Whenever I made it to the hospital to see Pete, he'd always say, 'I thought you weren't coming. Where have you been?' And I felt terrible that I hadn't been at his bedside, but I wasn't able to get to him till five or six and sometimes even eight o'clock at night because of filming. He couldn't even phone me, as his room didn't have a phone, so, for the first five days, no one could even speak to him, you could only talk to the nurses and find out how he was.

I wasn't in the right frame of mind to be filmed; I just wanted to be with Pete. All I cared about was him getting better. I was also really worried about the effect of the stress on our baby. The maternity ward was next to Pete's and I kept joking that I'd end up there soon because I was going to have the baby early because of the stress. I had never felt so knackered. I almost felt like I did when I had Postnatal Depression and everything had got too much for me. But I knew I wasn't depressed, it was complete exhaustion.

Finally, on Wednesday afternoon, the results of the lumbar puncture came back, confirming that Pete did have Viral Meningitis, an infection of the fluid in the spinal cord and the fluid that surrounds the brain. The doctors said that usually it only lasts three to four days and they were surprised that it had lasted for two weeks. Fortunately, it isn't such a serious infection like Bacterial Meningitis, which can result in brain damage or even death. It was such a relief to now know what was wrong with Pete, but he was still very weak. Then, thank God, he was moved from the depressing, tiny room he'd been in to a brand-new one with a nice shower and TV, which was like a room you'd expect in a private hospital.

So it seemed as if Pete was on the road to recovery, but by now I was at breaking point. I was still being filmed and I also had to deal with the paps when I visited Pete. When he had been in a week, I'd had enough of the attention. I couldn't even get to the main door because there were so many photographers outside and I really didn't want my pictures in the press just then, but the hospital didn't have the security to deal with them, only a few porters, because obviously this kind of thing doesn't usually happen. So I ended up driving across the grass to get to another door (luckily I have a 4x4) just to get away from them. Leaving Nicola to park the car, I scrambled across the passenger seat and ran through the door, and all the press could manage was a picture of my back. As I walked towards Pete's room,

I thought, *I can't take this anymore. I've got to have some time off.* I'd already told Roy how stressed I was and he had called Claire, telling her that he really thought I needed a break. The filming was continuing to put pressure on me. Pete was in hospital and that was our reality, that was what was going on in our lives and, of course, they wanted to film it, but I just wanted to be with Pete. I wanted to say, 'Give me a break! I'm a human being. Please stop leeching off me and sucking me dry, I want to be with my husband and I've got two kids to look after.' I'm sure anyone else would have been able to have time off work to be with their husband if he was as seriously ill as Pete, but I was expected to carry on. Finally I was given a few days off filming, so I could just concentrate on Pete. He was weak and I knew I had to protect him.

Pete had been in hospital for a week, and from his family only his brother Mike had come to see him. I felt that it would really cheer him up and help him recover if he saw his parents. Pete's mum and dad live in Cyprus, but I knew he would love to see them, and I felt that he needed his mum. I also knew that I could really do with some help, so I ended up calling Miranda, Pete's cousin. He is really close to her and I told her how concerned I was that no one had come to visit Pete. She told me that the family hadn't realised how ill Pete was and she promised to come down at the weekend, to help me with the children and to cook some meals for Pete, which I really appreciated. And then I thought, *I've got to speak to Savva, Pete's dad, and make sure he knows what the situation is.* I was completely honest about how I felt, saying how upset I was that no one had come to see him. Savva said he hadn't realised how unwell Pete was either. 'He's not on his death bed,' I answered, 'but he has been in hospital nearly a week, so he's really ill. If anyone's been in hospital for more than two days you know it's serious. I know he would love to see his family and I really need some help.' There, I'd had my say and I thought I was completely justified in it. To my relief, Savva promised that Thea, Pete's mum, would fly over with Debbie his daughter, Pete's sister. By the time they arrived, Pete was a hundred times better than he had been, though he was still very weak. His mum and sister were a great help when they arrived – his mum cooked lots of Pete's favourite food, because he really needed building up, and I felt some of the pressure was off me.

After what had seemed like the longest two weeks of my life, the doctors said that Pete could go home. But, the night before he was due to come out of hospital, he had a massive panic attack. Roy and Emma had come to see him to plan the next day's filming, but Pete said he felt sick and needed to sleep, so they left. Minutes after that he broke down and started crying. When I asked him what the matter was, he just said that he felt really strange. Then suddenly one side of his face seemed to droop and his hands began shaking uncontrollably as if he was having some kind of fit. It was really frightening seeing him like this. I rushed into the corridor and called for a doctor. The doctor thought he was having a panic attack brought on by stress of having been so ill. Also, Pete had read a horrible story in one of the papers about how he was supposed to have died, which really upset him, and I think it all got too much for him. Even though he was being discharged, the doctors kept saying that this did not mean he was better and that it was essential that he rested and took things easy. It could take weeks or months for him to fully recover.

Pete hadn't been filmed in his hospital bed but he

was filmed coming out of hospital. He looked so frail and weak and he kept getting out of breath whenever he tried to do anything. He was pale and he'd lost loads of weight – nearly two stone, which he didn't mind because he always worries about his weight! But I just wanted him to be strong again. Luckily, there was no press waiting outside the hospital – I don't know if Pete could have coped with being photographed. Back home, Junior was so excited to see him. He'd missed his dad so much. As soon as he saw Pete, he ran up to him and practically leapt into his arms and wouldn't let him go, and Harvey was just Harvey and smiled and laughed when he saw Pete. It was brilliant to have Pete back. I'd missed him so much and the house had felt so empty without him. Now I just wanted him to get well. I didn't want anything to upset him, so I was very protective of him when Roy was filming him. I wouldn't let him interview Pete; I just didn't think he was up to it.

During his stay in hospital, Pete had really missed his family and friends and he wanted us to have a barbeque at the weekend to catch up with everyone. I think he wanted to celebrate being home. But as it was only three days since he'd come out of hospital,

I wasn't at all sure it was such a good idea. But Pete insisted that he wanted a party and I thought he could probably do with some cheering up. We got caterers in, to take the pressure off us, and I was determined that Pete shouldn't overdo it. But the day didn't get off to a good start. In fact, Pete and me ended up having a massive row. It was all over something so trivial that blew out of proportion, probably because of the stress Pete had been under with his illness. I'd just changed Junior's nappy and noticed that he had quite bad nappy rash and he was understandably upset. Pete's mum had been the one changing him the last few times and I thought I'd better remind her and Pete to put Sudacream on when they changed him, which seemed to me a perfectly reasonable thing to ask. So I walked into the kitchen where everyone was sitting, picked up the pot of nappy rash cream and said casually, 'If anyone changes Junior, can you use this cream please. He's crying because his bum is sore.' And then I went back upstairs, thinking nothing of it. But Pete followed me and said, 'How dare you speak like this to my mum!' I was shocked and then angry that he could have a go at me when I was trying to do what was best for my child. 'He's my child too!' I shouted back. 'I don't give a shit about anyone else, I'm being a mum and if Junior's bum is sore and needs cream then I'll say it! You're always telling me that if I've got something to say to your parents then I should say it, so I have! I don't know what your problem is!'

Mike, Pete's brother, overheard us and even he said, 'Pete, I think you're being a bit out of order, Kate's said nothing wrong.' But Pete carried on having a go at me and, in the end, I'd had enough. I'd been so worried about him and so stressed the last couple of weeks, I couldn't take any more and I lost it. 'You can fuck off then and entertain your guests on your own!' I couldn't believe that we were arguing like this when Pete had only just come out of hospital, this was the last thing I wanted to happen. Then, just as quickly as it had begun, the row ended with Pete apologising. 'I'm sorry,' he said, 'I was picking at you for no reason. I know I'm still feeling ill, but I don't know what the matter is with me.'

'I'll tell you what the matter is,' I said, giving him a hug, 'We shouldn't be entertaining today, it's too much for you. And I'll tell you now, if I see you're getting stressed this afternoon, I'm going to make you come inside and have a rest.' While I knew it would be good for Pete to see his friends, I also knew that he should be taking it easy and I knew that I'd be the one who'd end up having to look after him when it all got too much. I was so close to giving birth and I really needed Pete to be strong. The last thing I wanted was for him to be too weak to be able to bond with the baby. That morning I saw a side to Pete I had never seen before. He was usually so laid back and it takes a lot to make him lose his temper. But, in the months following his illness, I was to see this side of Pete more and more. He became very short-tempered and argumentative with me, he had quite extreme mood swings and he would get very depressed. The doctors had warned us that having Meningitis can change a person's personality, so I just hoped that this was a temporary side-effect and that Pete would soon be back to his normal happy self.

We had also agreed that ITV could film footage of the barbeque and again I worried that it would be too much for Pete. Sure enough, halfway through the afternoon, when we had both been interviewed, I sensed that Pete wasn't feeling right. His eyes had gone all heavy again, just as they had before his last panic attack. When I walked into the kitchen, I found Pete sitting at the table, his head in his hands, not talking to his family, who were sitting round him drinking coffee. I put my arm round him and said, 'Pete, get in the other room now.'

'I'm fine,' he mumbled, but I knew he wasn't.

'I'm sorry everyone,' I said, 'but Pete needs to have some time on his own because he's not feeling well, so we're going into the other room.' The minute I got him into the lounge, he admitted that he didn't feel at all well and I could see that he was experiencing a panic attack. He asked me to get him some water, so I went back into the kitchen, where I told everyone, 'I'm really sorry, but Pete's not going to be able to spend any more time with you today. He's just not in a good way.' I went back to Pete to look after him and he was in a terrible state, crying and completely beside himself. It was awful to see – he's a man and yet he'd been made so weak and vulnerable by his illness, and I'd never seen him like this before. He was too frail and weak to entertain anyone, it had all been too much for his body; he needed more time to recover.

Later, when Pete had finally got over his attack, I

said to Claire, 'I told you that filming and interviewing Pete would be too much for him today. He
just can't cope. I know we've got more filming to do,
but I'd rather do most of it, even though I'm being a
stress-head myself, rather than put Pete through it.'
Later I found out from Pete that he had it in his head
that, because he'd been ill and hadn't been filming,
he needed to do some as soon as possible and that
was making him feel under pressure. I reassured him
that he didn't need to and he seemed to calm down as
he realised he really did need to take things easy.
Pete's illness had really put everything in perspective. It doesn't matter how successful your career is,
and how much money you earn, if you haven't got
your health and family, it means nothing.

CHAPTER FIFTEEN

COUNTDOWN TO THE BIRTH

All the way through my pregnancy I was so afraid of having another miscarriage, so worried that there'd be something wrong with the baby, and I was also paranoid that I'd get Postnatal Depression again. Unfortunately, you can suffer from it more than once, but I really hoped that I, and everyone close to me, would know the warning signs and I would get help straightaway. To protect myself, I decided I wanted things to be different when I gave birth this time.

Ideally, I wanted to have a natural birth, because I hadn't had a good experience when I had Junior by caesarean. I really wanted to enjoy my time with the new baby and, when you have a c-section, it does take longer to recover and it is really agonising after the operation. Not that I'm saying a natural birth is a walk in the park, I totally remember how sore I was down below after I'd had Harvey! But I ended up being booked in for a c-section on 29 June because the doctor said there was a small risk of my uterus rupturing if I went into labour naturally, having had a section so recently. However, I decided, after checking with the doctor, that if I went into labour before that date, I would try for a natural delivery. Partly because I wanted a natural birth, but also because of my absolute terror of having to have an epidural with such a large needle. I also had it in my head that having a caesarean might have been the cause of my Postnatal Depression, because I hadn't gone into labour and hadn't had to push the baby out – it felt a bit removed. Irrational, probably, but I couldn't help wanting a precise explanation for my depression.

When Junior was born, we'd hired a maternity

nurse because we both had work on just a few weeks after his birth and I thought it would help us both get some sleep, so that we wouldn't be stressing. Of course, the opposite happened, and I ended up getting Postnatal Depression and feeling that I hadn't bonded with Junior because I was surrounded by people and I never seemed to spend that precious one-to-one time with him. I had also invited Pete's family to stay with us straight after Junior was born and that hadn't been the right thing for me either. I needed time to bond with the baby, as any mother does. Suffering from Postnatal Depression and getting through it had taught me that I had to be honest about my feelings; it was no good bottling things up, so I explained how I felt to Pete and he completely supported me in what I wanted to do and I was upfront with his parents. I told them that I would like them to come over a week before the birth so they could spend time with us while I would still have the energy to entertain them and they could spend time with Junior and Harvey. Then I wanted them to be at the Portland on the day of the birth along with my family. But, when I went home, I wanted to be able to spend time with just the new baby and Pete, because I really wanted to bond with the baby and not go through what I did with Junior. I didn't want anyone to stay with us. I knew that I would be staying in hospital for four days and I decided to restrict the visiting hours on the advice of my doctor – not because I'm anti-social, but because I wanted as much time to bond with the baby as possible. I wanted the baby to stay next to me in the bed; I didn't want anyone else to feed her or change her nappy. I was going to sleep when the baby slept, instead of using the time to entertain visitors. I also decided that I was going to take eight weeks off work, because with Junior I had rushed back to work and I realised how bad that had been for both Junior and me. Once I had decided all this, I felt so much happier and I began looking forward to the birth. I no longer had that horrible tense feeling inside me, thinking that I was going to snap at people because they didn't understand how I felt and because I'd let all those negative feelings build up inside me.

* * *

Pete had been out of hospital for a couple of weeks and was getting stronger every day, though he had to take things easy. Meanwhile, the holiday house he'd had built in Cyprus was finally finished and we really wanted to buy furniture for it. Pete's dad had designed the house and had overseen its construction and, from the photographs he sent us, it looked amazing. While I was pleased that Pete was having the house built, as it would make the perfect holiday home, we did have a few rows about it. He said that I didn't seem interested in how the house was progressing. But I felt I hadn't been included in any of the design decisions – he had already decided what he wanted. Pete kept telling me to fly over to Cyprus and get involved in the design, but I couldn't, because I was working and I couldn't just leave the kids and fly over. I felt a little hurt that he hadn't asked me for my opinion. But, now it was time for the furniture and girlie touches, I thought I would make my mark. When I saw Dr Gibb for a check-up, I asked him when the latest date I could safely fly was. He told me I had up till 2 June, though he went on to say that he didn't actually advise me to fly at all unless it was urgent. I decided to go and that it had to be now or never; I wasn't going to leave it any later, and so I booked our flights for 17 May. We decided to go for three days. It would be a break and good to spend some time away as just the two of us, before our family became five . . . But, two days before we were due to fly out, I was doing a shoot for *Sunday* magazine to promote my novel, *Crystal*, and I felt really out of sorts. I kept getting out of breath and I couldn't stop yawning. I'd been experiencing this quite often during the pregnancy, but this was much worse. Just walking the short distance from the make-up room to where I was being photographed made me feel breathless. However, I didn't think it was anything serious and, on the day we were due to fly to Cyprus, I went shopping for some outfits to wear out there, as hardly any of my clothes fitted me anymore. When I got home, I tried on everything I'd bought in front of my mum, asking, as usual, whether I looked too big in what I was wearing. 'No, Kate,' she replied, rolling her eyes, as, like everyone else, she was bored with me asking the same question! Then I went and packed. I'm such an organised packer now, working out exactly what outfits I'm taking, along with matching accessories and shoes, so that, when I get to my destination, I know exactly what I'm going to wear during the day and in the evening.

Pete found out that our flight was delayed – instead of leaving at nine o'clock it would be midnight. He went off to a car showroom with his brother because he wanted to look at some sports cars, as we were going to go halves on one as a treat after his illness. I decided to have a lie down and sprawled out on my back on the bed like a starfish so I could stroke my belly and talk to the baby. I loved feeling the baby move. It was wonderful and weird as she was so active, making shapes against my belly – like the bit in *Alien,* but in a good way, obviously! But, after resting, I still didn't feel quite right and, as we drove to Heathrow, I was feeling anxious. *I hope I'll be okay when I'm away. I really don't want to go into labour in Cyprus and have the baby there . . .* Normally I'm a daredevil and would have thought, *Well, if I go into labour on the plane, it'll be fine, I can just write another chapter about it in my autobiography!* And, rightly or wrongly, that's my attitude sometimes. But now something was stopping me from feeling so confident and I wasn't at all sure that I wanted to get on the plane. So, even though it was half past nine at night, I phoned Dr Gibb. After apologising for disturbing him so late, I explained that I felt peculiar, not in any pain, just really odd. And he replied, 'Katie, I advise you not to fly.' And hearing that was the last straw – I needed someone to make my mind up for me. I told Pete how I felt and he immediately said that he didn't want to leave me and that he wouldn't go, but I told him I'd be fine. I thought that, after what Pete had been through with his illness, he could do with a break. 'Don't worry,' Pete told me as we said goodbye, 'I promise I'm not going to go out.'

'Pete, I really don't give a shit!' And I didn't. I trusted him to behave and, because I felt so odd, all I cared about was getting home to bed. And even though I was gutted because I couldn't choose the furniture with Pete, the prospect of having three days to chill was a good one.

However, I had such a strong nesting instinct and, instead of relaxing, I decided I had to get the house exactly the way I wanted it before the baby was born. I made a whole list of things I wanted to buy and the following morning I went shopping. My sister Sophie came into Brighton with me and I was still feeling incredibly out of breath, so much so that I had to park as close as I could to the escalator in the shopping centre, because I simply couldn't walk very far. I managed to make it to one shop to buy some lights but, as soon as I got inside, I felt so breathless that I had to ask for a chair so I could sit down. *What was going on?* I thought! *This isn't like me!* The other shop I wanted to go to was literally only a few minutes away, but I just didn't have the energy to walk there. I realised I had to get home. By the time I'd walked back to the car, I had a tingling sensation in my hands and above my mouth and the breathlessness was getting worse. When I drove home with my sister, I felt as if my vision was blurring slightly. Now I was getting scared and, as soon as I arrived home, I called the doctor and got an emergency appointment at the surgery.

The doctor checked me over and told me that one of my lungs didn't seem to be working properly and that I'd have to go straight to hospital. She suspected that I had a blood clot on my lung. She told me that this can be quite common during pregnancy and was completely treatable, but that didn't make me feel any better, as I was immediately worried because I didn't want this to affect the baby. Fortunately, my mum was with me, so she came to the hospital. I called Pete to let him know and he wanted to come back on the next flight, but I told him not to worry. I really didn't want to stress him, as he was still weak from his illness. I told him to stay and that I'd let him know what was happening. In the hospital I had to go to the maternity unit – right next to where Pete's ward had been. I'd joked about ending up here enough times when Pete was ill and now here I was. I was put on a heart monitor and the midwife tried to monitor the baby's heartbeat too, but she was being so active that they couldn't get one, but the fact that she was being so active was reassuring to me. The doctor told me they needed to run some blood tests to see how much carbon dioxide was in my blood and, even though I was worried about the prospect of a blood clot, I was panicking more about the needle, because of my phobia. The doctor tried one vein and couldn't get the needle in and it took twelve goes before they could finally get a vein. I was in a complete state by then but, just as I thought they'd finished taking blood and I could calm down, the doctor told me that they needed to take more.

'Why didn't you take all the blood the first time!' I exclaimed. 'You can see what I'm like about needles!' The doctor explained that they needed to take this sample from an artery vein. It took five different people to get a vein and at one point they were saying they would have to take it from a vein in my groin, but I begged them to do it from my arm and eventually they managed. I felt like a guinea pig, exactly like Pete and Harvey must have felt when they were in hospital.

Just when I thought things couldn't get any worse, the doctor said that they needed to give me an injection, because, if I did have a blood clot on my lung, they needed to treat it right away, but they couldn't tell for sure until the morning because only a chest X-ray would detect it and the X-ray department was shut for the night.

'Can't I discharge myself now and come back in the morning?' I asked, really wanting to go home. But they told me I had to stay and have the injection. 'Show me the needle,' I said, and it was slightly bigger than the one I use to give Harvey his daily injection. 'No, you can't do it to me!' I cried, overcome with panic. Every time the nurse tried to give me the injection I'd say 'No, no, no!' over and over again. Then I'd calm down and tell the nurse she could go ahead, but, as soon as I felt the needle on my skin again, I'd panic and shout 'No, stop!' just like a little kid.

'Come on, Kate, you need to have this injection done! Grow up!' My mum urged me, but that didn't help.

'Shut up, Mum! You wouldn't like it if it was you!' I shot back at her.

And inside I was thinking, *Can't I just have the baby now? I really don't know if I can go through all this* . . . Finally, my mum told me she was going to go to the loo and, by the time she came back, she wanted the injection to have been done. I gave up and let the nurse do it, wincing all the time. I'm going to have to go to my therapist to see if she can help me overcome my phobia of needles, otherwise God knows what the birth's going to be like.

The results of the blood tests came back and the doctor said it was one of two things, either I was hyperventilating or it was a blood clot. I couldn't believe I was hyperventilating that much, but then maybe I was, as I'd got myself into such a state when they tried to take blood. As it had been such a performance getting blood the first time, they kept a cannula needle in my arm, so they wouldn't have to find a vein again if they needed to take more blood. Feeling the cannula in my arm, I felt very sorry for myself, like an animal with an injured paw. I needed to stay overnight, so I was put in a side room – right next to the maternity ward where women had just given birth. I was told that I would have to pay for the room and it would be £80–£100. I was outraged! 'I'm in an NHS hospital and I don't even want to be here, it's the doctors who want me to stay in, so why do I have to pay, isn't that what I pay my taxes for?' I said to mum in disgust. The room didn't even have its own loo. But the staff did look after me really well, so I can't complain on that score. All night I kept hearing the different cries of all the newborn babies and I thought, *I've got to get used to this!* And I stroked my belly thinking, *I wish the baby would come now – it seems I've got to wait ages.*

My mum returned to the hospital in the morning and, finally, around one o'clock, I was wheeled down to the X-ray department, ironically by the same porters who had wheeled Pete around the hospital when he was ill. God, I felt like our family had had enough of hospitals to last a lifetime . . . I had to go through the whole needle ordeal again as the doctor said they needed to give me another injection. Immediately I started playing up, saying, 'Look, I've got this cannula in, why don't you do the injection there?' But the doctor insisted they needed to do it in another vein and I was crying like a baby as he tried to find one. I felt a sharp pain as the needle went in. 'Have you done it,' I said, wincing. But he said he couldn't find a vein.

'Please,' I begged him, 'I can't go through this again, my arms are really hurting.' And so the doctor ended up doing the injection in the cannula. I wish he'd done that in the first place.

I had to wait all day for the results and, when they came back, I was relieved to find out that I didn't have a blood clot on my lung, instead I was seriously anaemic again and my haemoglobin levels were very low, at 8.2 when they should be around 13. A level of 8 means you have to have a blood transfusion. This low level was the most likely cause of my breathlessness. I was given two choices by the doctor: either I could go to the hospital three times a week to be given an iron injection or I could be put on a drip for six hours now and be given the entire dose. They'd seen what I was like with needles, so they thought it was probably best if I had the drip. I wasn't going to argue with that – there was no way I could have coped with that number of injections. I had been eating really healthily throughout this pregnancy, with lots of iron-rich food, but the doctor said that, unfortunately, babies are like parasites and they take all the nutrients and iron from you. The doctor said that they couldn't believe I hadn't passed out because I was so anaemic and, if I had flown to Cyprus, I would almost certainly have fainted, so thank God I didn't get on the flight. I had to wait for an hour after I'd finished on the drip, as it was such a high dose of iron, just to make sure I didn't have a reaction, and by then Pete had arrived at the hospital.

It was so good to see him, but I felt really sorry for him because he'd flown all the way to Cyrpus only to fly straight back again. It only goes to show what a good man he is. As he drove us home, I said 'What is it with us? There's always a drama!' Drama I could do without.

Throughout my pregnancy, I hadn't wanted to find out the sex of our baby, I wanted it to be a surprise. I had found out the sex when I was pregnant with Junior and I thought there might be less chance of getting Postnatal Depression if I did the opposite with this pregnancy. But because 2007 had been a year with so many stresses, I suddenly thought I would like to find out whether we were having a boy or a girl. 'What do you think, Pete?' I asked. 'Shall we find out on our next scan?' He was up for it and that night in bed when I stroked my belly and felt the baby move, I whispered, 'I can't wait to find out what you are.' Deep down I knew I wanted a girl. Of course, I would be happy to have a boy too – the only thing that mattered was that the baby was healthy.

* * *

It was the moment of truth, it was my birthday and I was having my scan. I was lying on the couch and Dr Gibbs was holding the ultrasound device on my belly. *Please be a girl,* I was thinking, looking at my baby on the screen. 'Well, Katie, I'm going to make you very happy. You're having a baby girl.'

'Oh really?!' I gasped. 'That's brilliant!' And it was the best birthday present I have ever had, that and Pete proposing to me on my birthday (I'd better say that or he will get the hump!). I had so wanted a girl this time because I had lost a baby girl when I miscarried. When we came out of the room we were being filmed for our reality show and I exclaimed, 'I can have another pink room in the house!' I was so excited by the news, but anxious as well. Having a girl was a dream come true to me, as I'd always wanted a girl, and inside I worried that it was almost too good to be true and something would go wrong . . . Pete was great at reassuring me as he always is, though, and the scan was completely normal, so I tried not to worry.

I wanted to go shopping straightaway to buy baby girl clothes. I couldn't wait to dress her up in pink and go to town with the glitter and bling because I love my girly things so much. Of course, I love dressing my boys, but it's not quite the same. And I said, 'You will never see a baby girl dressed in as much bling and pinked out as much as mine will be!' Pete just shrugged. He knows what I'm like and he was as happy as me about the news. But I couldn't hit the shops as I had interviews to do and I had to find a dress for some TV awards and so the rest of my birthday was spent charging round London, in and out of boutiques. The episode they showed on TV looked as if I'd only gone for my scan and then driven home again and that I was being a right moody cow, but it didn't show all the other things I'd done in London that day. I'd actually been really busy and I'd had no time to get ready for the birthday meal Pete had organised. It put me in a vile mood, I admit. When you're pregnant you never feel your best anyway and all I wanted was some time to have a shower, do my make-up, feel relaxed and enjoy seeing my family and friends.

By the time we pulled up at the restaurant, Pete and me were rowing. He was cross because I had kept him waiting and because I was moaning about being filmed when I didn't look good. I ended up getting out of the car and walking into the restaurant on my own, leaving Pete to let rip to the cameras. And when I saw the episode back, he really had, saying that I was the hardest person to live with, how he'd never had as much stress in his life as he'd had with me. Even Pete was shocked by how angry he'd been when he saw the show. When we're arguing, we never hold back, not even when we're being filmed. But it didn't bother me. He's told me before that I'm the hardest woman ever to live with, but he's still here, isn't he? And when he says things like that I always wind him up and say, 'You know where the door is, don't you?' That's just what we're like. We say terrible things to each other, but we get over it because we love each other so much and because we're married with kids. Within minutes of Pete coming into the restaurant we'd kissed and made up. And I loved his birthday present to me – first-class tickets for the whole family to fly to Australia for Christmas. I also thought it would be nice to have a birthday when I'm not pregnant in the future, as I've been pregnant on my birthday for the last three years!

CHAPTER SIXTEEN

CHAOS AND CRYSTAL

Now I knew I was having a girl, I could start thinking about names. I knew exactly what I wanted to call her – Princess, because to me she would be my little princess, doubly precious because of the baby girl I'd lost. She might get picked on at school for her name, but then you can just as easily get picked on for wearing the wrong trainers and I think I can get away with giving my daughter an unusual name. But when I told my mum, she rolled her eyes and said straightaway, 'How on earth can you call her that! That's so cruel! What about when she's older.'

'She could grow up to be a butch lesbian with a shaved head!' I replied, 'But then it's up to her to change her name.' I changed mine when I was eighteen from Katrina Amy Alexandria Alexis Infield Price to simply Katie Price, so my mum was a fine one to talk after giving me a mouthful of a name like that.

I was also honest with Pete's parents about what we were going to call the baby. One of the things that had seriously stressed me out when I was pregnant with Junior had been the way Pete and me had rowed so badly over what to call him. Pete had it in his head that he had to call our son Savva, after his dad, because it's the Greek-Cypriot tradition that you name your first son after your dad and your first daughter after your mum. But much as I liked Pete's dad, I didn't want to call my son Savva, as it just wasn't a name I was happy with. I'm not Greek-Cypriot, so I didn't think I should have to follow a tradition that's got nothing to do with me. It wasn't until Pete and me both came up with the name Junior and decided to give him Savva as his middle name

On our way to the airport, leaving
Belize where we'd been on holiday.

Travelling in style
for an *OK!* photo shoot to celebrate our
first wedding anniversary.

Even when I was heavily pregnant,
I didn't stop my work. I was proud
to be able to tell the world I was
expecting a baby girl.

In the back garden
at home.

In America.

I love being able to dress Princess Tiáamii up in lots of pretty pink.

My beautiful daughter, Princess Tiàami, was born on 29th June 2007.
Here we are together in Cyprus.

In Cyprus with
my family.

Top left: A picnic in the garden with Harvey.

My other loves: my horses, Jelly and Tyke, and my pink cars.

Me with Tyke at home.

Junior looking cool just like his dad.
Maybe he'll be a pop star one day too?

With my gorgeous daughter on holiday.

These were the pictures that launched our golden handcuffs deal with ITV.

that the row was sorted, and it was stress I didn't need this time round. So, just after we discovered we were having a girl, I decided to call Pete's parents and let them know the name I was thinking of. I spoke first to Thea, asking her if she knew how much Pete and me had argued about choosing Junior's name. She hadn't known and was really shocked and immediately wanted to know why.

'I've been brought up the way I have and Pete's been brought up the way he has,' I replied, 'and I understand that your culture's different to mine, and I'm not knocking it, but you've also go to remember I'm not going to be following your traditions because I'm not Greek-Cypriot. To me it's strange that your tradition would expect me to name my baby after you when you've already got a granddaughter called Thea.'

I was really glad that I was upfront with his mum and I think she understood how I felt and appreciated my honesty. She knows what I went through with my Postnatal Depression and is very sympathetic. And I want Pete's parents to understand my feelings; otherwise it puts a strain on me and Pete. He obviously doesn't want to upset his mum and dad and worries that he will by not following their traditions. His parents were fine about it, though. It was Pete who had the problem and he really wanted us to call the baby Thea. Because we didn't name Junior after Pete's dad, he really wanted to name his daughter after his mum this time. We didn't argue like we had over Junior's name, but it was becoming an issue between us and I thought, *Oh no, here we go again!* At the end of the day, I was the one carrying the baby, and I wanted to have a say. 'What about Princess Thea?' I suggested. 'You'll be letting my mum down if we don't call the baby Thea as her first name,' Pete insisted, and I was really upset at his attitude, as this was my baby we were talking about. I thought I'm not going to have this argument every time I have a baby. I decided to go for the direct approach again and so I phoned his mum and dad up. 'Pete seems to think that you've got a problem because I didn't name Junior after you, Savva,' I told Pete's dad. 'And now he wants to call the baby Thea, but I want to call her Princess.'

Savva was really nice about it and said, 'Don't worry about Peter. All that matters is that the baby is healthy.' And I spoke to Thea as well, explaining that we were arguing about the baby's name again and she reassured me that she really didn't mind if the baby wasn't named after her, though I did say that I was thinking about calling her Princess Thea. Later, they phoned Pete and had a go at him for stressing me out, telling him that they really didn't mind what we called the baby. Pete is really protective of his parents, so he was cross with me for phoning them. But at least I'd sorted things out and stopped the arguments.

Then Pete came up with the great idea of combining both our mum's names – straightaway I loved the idea, because it would make our daughter's name unique and it would mean something special to us. One night, when my brother Daniel was round at the house with his wife Louise, we all wrote down different versions of the name to see how we could spell it. I think it was my brother who came up with Tiàamii – it's pronounced tee-ah-me. I loved the name because I thought it looked really pretty and unusual. I was determined that no one should shorten her name to Tia. She would be Princess or Princess Tiàamii.

* * *

Typically for me, I couldn't take it easy now I was only a few weeks away from the birth. I had to promote my new novel, *Crystal* – the story of a beautiful and talented singer in a girl band who shoots to stardom after winning a reality TV talent show, but falls for the wrong man. This one mistake could cost her everything: her friendships, her fame and her chance of ever finding love again. It's a page-turner, I promise! I was launching the book in spectacular style at Harrods, followed by interviews and book signings. Some of the signings were a very long way away from home and from my London hospital and, while I might say cockily 'Oh it will be okay if I go into labour on my book signings! It'll be something to remember!' inside I was panicking. Still, everything else seemed to be going okay for once. Pete was still fragile, but he was getting stronger every day. Harvey's leg was continuing to make progress too and Junior was really excited about having a baby sister.

On bank holiday Monday at the end of May, Pete and I decided to drive to Toys 'R' Us to choose birthday presents for Harvey and Junior. We'd already given Harvey some presents, as his birthday had been at the weekend but Junior's was in a couple of weeks' time and we wanted to give the boys a joint party. Up till then, because of Pete's illness, we hadn't had much time to organise anything. We were both feeling really happy as we drove back, pleased with all the toys we'd ordered, imagining how much the boys would love them, when we got a phone call. Pete took it and immediately I could tell that something was very wrong. It was a paramedic. There had been an accident at home and a mirror had fallen on Harvey and injured him. 'Is he all right?' I asked anxiously. I couldn't believe that Harvey had been hurt again. I knew I had to stay calm and so I spoke to the paramedic, explaining about Harvey's medical condition and how he would need his emergency cortisone injection. I was desperate to get home, but we were stuck behind Sunday afternoon drivers who were driving painfully slowly and I couldn't overtake because we were on narrow country roads. To make matters worse, we'd chosen to go in our new Ferrari and it was raining and I was having to drive very cautiously, as those cars can wheel spin in wet conditions and that was the last thing I needed.

My stomach lurched when I saw the ambulance

parked in our driveway. *Please let him be okay,* I prayed, as I got out of the car. Harvey was lying on a stretcher in the back of the ambulance. He had several deep gashes on his face, which was covered in blood, and his nose looked badly swollen. He didn't seem to be breathing, his eyes were closed and for a few heart-wrenching seconds I thought he was dead, 'Oh my God, is he okay?' I exclaimed to the paramedic, feeling as if my legs were about to give way with shock. He replied that they had to get him to the hospital as soon as possible. Knowing how vital it was that Harvey had his cortisone injection, I rushed inside the house to get the bag containing all his medication. I couldn't believe the state of the hallway, there was blood everywhere and the huge Venetian glass mirror was lying shattered on the carpet. *He could have been killed,* I thought, a wave of horror rushing through me. I quickly gathered Harvey's things and went back outside. The nanny was sitting in the ambulance, clutching a cloth to her nose and looking dazed. When I asked her if she was okay, she seemed out of it and I thought she must have concussion. I asked her what had happened and she said that she'd been sitting in the hallway with

Harvey as he played with his toys. Suddenly she saw the mirror falling towards him, so she dived in front of him to save him from being hit, but he had been struck by some pieces of glass. There were so many questions I wanted answering but Harvey was my priority and I got in the ambulance with him, though I felt a horrible sense of déjà vu as it drove us to the hospital. I sat next to Harvey, holding his hand, but he wasn't talking and he wasn't moving. I didn't know whether he was in shock or whether he had concussion. It was really frightening seeing him like this. We were taken to my local hospital – the same one that Harvey had been taken to after his burn accident and the same one from where someone had reported me to Social Services, a place I'd hoped I'd never have to go to again. Once Harvey was wheeled inside, it was the all-too familiar routine of having to explain to each and every doctor about his medical condition and about what dosage of medication he needed. Honestly, you'd have thought if you told one doctor they could explain it to the others.

By now Harvey was really upset and crying because he was in so much pain, especially when the nurses cleaned the deep cuts on his face. I hated seeing him suffer again. But he is such a tough, brave little boy that very soon he was calm, accepting that he had to lie down and be still. The hospital was really busy and, when Harvey was wheeled along the corridor to have an X-ray to see if he had broken his nose, I could sense everyone staring as they recognised us. On top of my anxiety for Harvey, I felt embarrassed too. I hated people thinking that I might have been responsible in any way for Harvey's injuries.

The doctors told me that they couldn't treat Harvey there because of his medical condition and so, at six o'clock the following morning, he would have to be transferred to Croydon, where his cuts could be stitched – I was told that the wounds could be left open for twenty-four hours. My heart sank at the thought of Harvey having to stay in hospital yet again. He had been through so much this year. Meanwhile, the nanny had been discharged within an hour; she didn't have concussion, just a small cut on her nose.

At Croydon Hospital the following day Harvey was given another X-ray and this time it was discovered that he had broken his nose, so my opinion of my local hospital sank even lower, because they had told me earlier that he hadn't. He was going to be operated on that afternoon and then have his nose re-set and his cuts stitched. I was immediately worried because he was going to be given a general anaesthetic, something which we were told wouldn't have been safe when he was being treated for his burn injury. But the doctors explained that this time Harvey's condition was more stable. I had to show the surgeon a picture of Harvey so he could see what his nose was supposed to look like. Harvey wasn't allowed to eat or drink anything, which was hard for him as he is so used to his routine and he couldn't understand why he couldn't have anything to eat. Not being able to drink anything affects his medication too, as he has to keep his water levels up. He got upset and started throwing himself back and it was really difficult to calm him down.

As he was wheeled down to theatre, with me at his side, we had to endure more curious stares from people. I was allowed in the operating theatre with Harvey and he was so incredibly good, just lying there quietly. It brought tears to my eyes watching him. He's so innocent, and he doesn't understand what's going on, he just trusts me that everything is going to be all right. Then the anaesthetist put the mask on him and Harvey started to drift into unconsciousness and it was so horrible, because it looked like he was dead. 'I love you, Harvey,' I said, holding his hand, and he murmured groggily back, 'Love you too, Mummy.' As I left him there, I felt overwhelmed with emotion, imagining the worst – that he wouldn't wake up and that I'd lose my little boy. The next forty-five minutes were the longest ever . . . Finally, to my huge relief, a nurse came and told me that the operation had gone well, and I was taken to the recovery room to wait for Harvey. As he came round he was fine, his cuts had been stitched and his nose had Steri-Strips across it, and he must have been feeling okay because as soon as we got back to the room he asked for something to eat, which he wasn't allowed for the next half hour. I thought that after a couple of hours he would be discharged and I'd be able to take him home, but they wanted to keep him another night to monitor his condition. By now I was almost beside myself with exhaustion, but I couldn't ask Pete to take my place alongside Harvey, as he was still recovering from his Meningitis and was still really weak.

It was such a relief when Harvey was discharged from hospital the following day. He was so happy to be back home with the family. I wanted to rest, so I was on good form for my *Crystal* book launch but we had a bit of a childcare problem that meant I couldn't stay in London the night before appearing on the Chris Moyles show and there was no way I could leave Pete to look after the kids in his present fragile state. I would have to leave first thing in the morning after I had creamed and re-bandaged Harvey's leg, changed the dressings on his face, given him his medication and got him and Junior ready for school. On the morning of the launch I was up at the crack of dawn. By now I was just a few weeks away from giving birth and I was exhausted. But I was still in the car, leaving the house at quarter to six, which should have given me plenty of time to get to Radio 1 for my live interview at eight. However, we got caught in horrendous traffic, which delayed us. I had the radio on and could hear Chris Moyles and his gang slagging me off, speculating whether I was going to get there on time or not. Chris was saying, 'Shall I let her on?' And I thought, *Come on guys, give me a break! I'm a few weeks away from having a baby, I've got two kids*

to look after, a husband who's still fragile after a
major illness and no one to help me at the moment.
Yes, you should be on time for things, but sometimes
shit happens . . . I would only have been fifteen
minutes late and, even though my management had
called the production team to let them know that, at
eight o'clock, Moyles said that he wouldn't let me on
air. I'd always got on well with Chris before that, but
I didn't need his power trips. I felt like saying, *Come*
to my house one morning and look after Harvey and
I'll present your show and then you'll see what I have
to do.

* * *

I didn't let it get to me, though, as I had a busy launch
day ahead. 'You're not going to drop me, are you?' I
joked to the four strapping lads who were carrying
me as I sat in my jewel-shaped sedan chair like a
princess, dressed in a flowing white dress encrusted
with silver crystals and wearing a sparkling tiara on
my head that spelling out *Crystal*. Yes, this was me
on my way to launch my second novel. Never let it be
said that I make an understated entrance! I'd, of
course, had the idea to arrive like this for my book

signing at Harrods and so far everything was going to plan: the sun was shining, and in front of me I could see a sea of photographers and crowds of fans lining the pavement. The lads – who were stripped to the waist with *Crystal* written across their backs and chests – lowered me down carefully and then I posed away for the photographers. When they'd got their shots, I was led inside Harrods. Panpipe players were playing in front of me as I walked through the store and up the escalators to where the signing was going to be taking place. And I was being followed by hundreds of people, as if I was the pied piper. It was such fun and I felt like royalty, especially since I was wearing this amazing dress. I know people often see me looking shit on my reality show, with no make-up on and wearing a tracksuit, but at my signings I really like to make an effort. After the launch I managed two days of book signings, but by then I was exhausted and really suffering with sciatica. When I saw Dr Gibb for a check-up, he said I could go into labour at any time. Suddenly the thought of going into labour miles away from home was really terrifying. I hated letting people down and felt really guilty, but I had to cancel the rest of my signings. I love doing them, but

I wanted to be feeling my best. I decided to do them later in the year. Meanwhile, *Crystal* was doing brilliantly and had gone straight to number one.

So now I had just under three weeks before my caesarean on 29 June and, much as I wanted to take it easy, Pete and me still had a childcare crisis on our hands. We contacted several agencies and interviewed lots of nannies and some we even tried out, but it was so hard finding the right person, someone who would be able to cope with Harvey's special needs as well as look after Junior. I wanted a nanny to fit in with our family. And I hated having to interview would-be nannies in my house, as it felt like a real invasion of my privacy. Fortunately, though, within a week we found one nanny who seemed great, but we still needed to find another one too, as I really wasn't sure about leaving her to look after both boys when I had the baby. Meanwhile I was driving Pete mad with my nesting! I could not stop cleaning and organising the house – I'd never been like this with my other pregnancies. I was obsessed with getting everything ready for the baby's arrival – hanging up all her clothes in her wardrobe, packing the baby bag, then unpacking it to check I'd got everything. I spent ages sticking crystals onto her baby blankets and baby gros. I wanted her to be able to look at those early pictures of herself and think, *Wow! Look at all those crystals on me!* I also threw a joint baby shower with Claire, my manager, whose baby was due a few weeks after mine, which was such good fun. We held it in a marquee in my garden and it had an Alice in Wonderland theme, with a Mad Hatter's table and oversized chairs and thrones, a clairvoyant, magician and a poker table with a proper dealer. I also had goody bags, which were packed with treats, including pole dancing lessons, make-up and lots of gorgeous toiletries for all the guests, and I think I was just as excited about handing them out as I was about the party. So while I was still stressing over childcare, there were lots of positive things going on in my life as well. Above all, I was so excited about meeting my little Princess.

CHAPTER SEVENTEEN

OUR PRINCESS!

'Hello Princess,' I whispered softly, as I held my newborn daughter in my arms. She was just a few hours old and I couldn't stop gazing at her as she slept, taking in her delicate skin, her tiny hands and her incredibly long eyelashes. Junior has long lashes, but Princess's looked as if they were even longer. I was surprised by her colouring, imagining that she would be dark like Junior, but she was quite fair, with a hint of ginger. I'm not sure quite where she got that from. Maybe from my side, as my nan had auburn hair. As she was so new, she was still a bit scrunched up. I always think that newborn babies look like little old men; they need a few weeks to grow into themselves. But she was perfect and she was so peaceful as she slept. *Oh my God,* I thought, *I've got a baby girl!* And I felt such intense love for her that I just didn't want to put her down. I had a deep feeling of happiness and calm inside me. As soon as she was born I felt as if all the bad feelings and emotions I'd had with my depression had finally left me. And I felt that I could put all the tough times we'd had recently behind me because our beautiful new baby was here.

Her birth had gone so well and had been such a positive experience. It was all so different from when I had Junior. With him, because of my needle phobia, I had ended up having gas and air to cope with the epidural, but that left me feeling so out of it and sick that I could barely take in the fact that I had just had a baby as Junior was handed to me. But with Princess I had been mentally preparing myself by seeing the anaesthetist, who explained exactly what having the epidural would involve, and by seeing my therapist. And when it came to having the epidural, it was all over so quickly and didn't even hurt. 'Oh my God!' I exclaimed to Pete, 'I can't believe I made all that fuss for nothing!' I was completely with it for Princess's delivery and I loved it. It was so wonderful when she was handed to me and she lay on my chest, her newborn skin touching mine. I immediately thought, *This is so amazing. I want to have another baby straightaway!* I also knew that everyone around me wanted me to bond with Princess, as I heard Dr Gibb tell the midwife to lay the baby on me, whereas Pete held Junior first. When Dr Gibb had finished stitching me, I was wheeled into the recovery room, Princess still lying on me. There I was looked after by a very pretty nurse and I thought, *Pete, please don't fancy her!* But then I was the one with his baby, wasn't I? Finally I was wheeled back to my room, where my family and Pete's mum and dad and our friends were waiting. With Junior I had felt overwhelmed by being surrounded by so many visitors and I remember my feeling of helplessness as I let everyone hold him. But with Princess I had made my feelings clear and so had the doctors – I was not to have many visitors, and, if I did, they were not to stay long. So, within five minutes of me arriving back at my room and everyone seeing the baby, they left, with the exception of Pete's mum and dad, who stayed a little bit longer. I was happy to have them there because they live in Cyprus and won't see as much of their granddaughter as my family.

This time I didn't let anyone hold her, as I just wanted to bond with her and that was all that mattered. I knew from the moment that she was handed to me that I had though. I spent those four days in The Portland just holding her in my arms and gazing at her, blissfully happy. I was the one who fed her and changed her, and I slept when she did. She went to the night nursery, though, because I thought it would be sensible to try to get some sleep, so that I could properly recover from my caesarean, but, as soon as I woke up in the morning, I'd phone the midwife and ask them to bring her to me straightaway and I would be so excited about seeing her again. I've already mentioned that I'd stuck crystals over her clothes, but she turned out to be bigger than I'd expected so none of the special sparkly baby gros actually fitted her. I'd just have to get started on her other clothes when I went home, but at least her blankets were blingtastic!

I couldn't help noticing that Pete wasn't quite as emotionally involved with her as he had been with Junior. He still cried at her birth, as he always does when he's moved, but he seemed to be holding back slightly. With Junior he had spent hours holding him, gazing at him, and had been completely fascinated by his son, and yet he didn't do this with Princess. I became paranoid that he might have depression when he kept saying Princess's birth felt so different to Junior's because he had been his first. But maybe he was scared that I would get Postnatal Depression again if he did too much. Maybe he was holding back to give me time to bond? I knew that I didn't have depression, though. I felt so good inside, so strong, and happy. I was back to the old me, the me I had been before I got pregnant with Junior; the Kate that Pete had fallen in love with. It seemed that strong, happy Kate had been away for so long.

We did have a few visitors, mind you. In fact, I wanted my family to come up and see me, but my mum wouldn't as she said she wanted me to have that time with the baby. And it was ironic, because this time I really wanted to show off the baby and for everyone to see how happy I was. But I guess they were just being protective because, when I had Junior, I'd pretended to be okay and I wasn't. So when I said I was fine this time round, they must have wondered if I really was. One of my visitors asked to hold Princess as soon as she saw her in my arms and she was taken aback when I replied, 'I'm sorry you can't hold her.'

'Why not?' she replied, looking really surprised.

'I'm sorry, but, because of my Postnatal Depression last time, I'm not ready to let people hold her yet; I've got to make sure that I've bonded with her.' And I was pretty angry that I was having to explain myself, as everyone who was close to me knew what I'd been through and knew how I wanted things to be this time, yet she didn't seem to take in what I was saying.

'You weren't that bad, give her here.'

'No, you're not holding her, that's final!' I said, and inside I felt really good that I was saying what I felt. I didn't care what anyone else thought, I was thinking about me and the baby. The day after Princess was born, I was ready to let Pete's mum and dad hold her, but I kept having to tell myself, *Just let them hold her and don't be silly, they're not going to take her away from you.* The important thing for me was that I felt I was in control; I was the one saying to his parents that they could hold her. But I wouldn't let anyone else apart from Pete feed or change her. I wanted to do everything for her myself. It was probably hard for Pete that I was the one making all the rules, but as he didn't want me to get depression again, he fully understood.

Unfortunately, during this time Pete's dad became very unwell. He'd recently had an operation and was feeling sick and weak. He looked awful and none of the doctors he saw seemed to know what was wrong with him. There had even been a question mark over whether he and Thea would have been able to fly over for the birth at all, but I had persuaded them, saying that I really wanted them to see their grand-daughter. I also wanted them to be there for Pete and to show them that I wasn't feeling like I had with Junior. The arrangement was that they would see the baby while I was in The Portland and then, when I went home, they would fly back to Cyprus, because I'd decided I wasn't going to have any visitors at home this time. As Pete's dad seemed to get worse, more and more of Pete's attention and time was taken up with him, which I understood. I tried to help and support Pete, but, at the same time, I'd just had my baby girl and I really needed to focus on her. I wasn't being selfish, I just didn't want to get Postnatal Depression again. So while I was staying in The Portland, Pete spent quite a lot of time taking his dad to the doctors. I also knew that if my mum or stepdad were ill, I'd be behaving in just the same way, wanting to get them the best treatment. At times I felt he was a little distant with me when we were together, but then I thought, *Come on, it's his dad, he's bound to be worried.* And actually it just meant that I could spend even more time on my own with Princess, which I loved. I was so looking forward to going home, to spending time with the new baby, Pete and the boys. Junior had seen her at the hospital (Harvey couldn't because he had school) and he was completely entranced by her, wanting to kiss her and cuddle her, and being incredibly gentle.

* * *

'I really don't care what *that* thinks. Dad is my first priority and I'm going to deal with it. If they need to come here then they can.' I was lying on the bed, Princess beside me, and I couldn't help overhearing

Pete on the phone to his brother Mike. I felt as if I'd
been hit, he was referring to me as *that* and planning
to bring his parents to our house even though he knew
I didn't want visitors because I desperately didn't
want to get Postnatal Depression again. What's more,
he'd deliberately made the call so I could hear. I burst
into tears, hurt and angry. *How fucking dare you!* I
thought. *I'm lying here with your baby, and I've just
had major surgery, so I'm really sore and I can hardly
move.* Up till then I'd felt in control of everything to
do with the baby and I was really happy. But I was
still anxious. All I wanted to do was concentrate on
Princess and be with Pete and the boys.

But, upset as I was, I couldn't lose it with Pete. He
was under pressure. I knew he was really stressed
about his dad, he hadn't fully recovered from
Meningitis and now he had a new baby to bond with.
I knew that I was so close to Princess and I didn't
want him to feel left out. 'I heard what you said on
the phone, Pete,' I called out. 'What do you mean
about me not being your first priority?'

'I've got to look after my dad,' he replied, walking
back into the bedroom.

'Pete, the best place for him is seeing a specialist in

London, not down here with country doctors.' I answered, trying to stay calm.

'Look,' Pete went on, 'he's just collapsed; I don't want him going to some crap London hospital. I want him here.' I was trying to be reasonable, thinking that I would want to do exactly the same if it was my mum or stepdad, and that Pete wasn't in the wrong for wanting his dad here. I took a deep breath and suggested that, when Pete's parents came to the house, that they stayed in the guest cottage. That way we could all have some privacy; they would be welcome to stay there as long as they wanted and I wouldn't feel overwhelmed by visitors so soon after I'd had Princess.

So they did come and stay and I was really fine about it. They stayed in the guest cottage and came over to the house for meals and to watch TV. And I was spending most of the time in my bedroom, resting with Princess. I was so much more comfortable there because I could lie down and I had everything there that I needed: the baby's milk, her clothes and nappies. Princess was sleeping in our bedroom. I hadn't even finished decorating hers, as I didn't quite know what I wanted to do with it and I wanted something really special. Her crib was beside our bed but, in fact, I had her in bed with me at night, because she would settle better next to me and because I was so sore it was easier to have her there. I knew I was breaking all the rules, but I didn't care. I was loving this time with her and I wanted to have her close to me all the time. I was so content in my own little world with Princess that I didn't go downstairs very often. I think Pete took it the wrong way and thought that I was avoiding his parents. 'I would tell you if that was the case,' I told him. The truth was I just wanted to be with Princess. It had been a big step to have her in the room with me – I hadn't done this with Junior.

Looking back, maybe I should have come down and seen if his parents were okay more often than I did. Pete was understandably focusing on his dad, because he really wasn't well. He looked terrible, jaundiced and frail, and he really wasn't himself. Pete had taken him to see different doctors and to the hospital, but no one seemed to know what was wrong. It was putting Pete under severe stress, but I did feel a bit neglected. When you've just had a baby you are vulnerable and need support, and a caesarean is a major operation – it takes several weeks to recover. Also, when I went downstairs, things felt slightly tense. I sensed that his parents were uncomfortable about staying when I'd just had the baby because they knew about my Postnatal Depression and they also knew how I'd been advised by the doctors not to have any visitors. But they loved looking at the baby and holding her, which I was completely fine with this time because I made sure that I was the one in control. Rather than feeling that she was being taken away from me, I would ask his parents if they wanted to hold her. I wasn't playing games: I knew what was right for me and for the baby. Pete would sometimes comment, 'They just want to hold her!' implying that I was making a big deal about it, and inside I'd think, *Don't try and make me let them hold her.* So I was honest and said, 'I'm sure you don't want me to be ill again, so please just let me do this my way.' Now I'm happy to let other people hold her because I know I've completely bonded with her, but back then I was so anxious that I had to do things my way. There was just one moment when Princess was in her baby bouncer and Pete's mum went over to her and I was suddenly gripped by that horrible paranoid feeling I'd had with Junior of *Get off my baby! Don't touch her!* which I know is ridiculous. *Shit*, I thought, *Not this again*, so I casually said that I was going to take her back upstairs for her nap. Because I stayed in control, the feeling that his mum was going to take my baby away from me went as quickly as it came.

It was so lovely seeing Junior with his baby sister. He completely adored her and, when he got back from nursery, she was the first person he'd ask to see. He loved helping me look after her, and he kept calling her his 'bister', because he couldn't say sister, which was so cute. I felt that having another baby really helped strengthen my bond with him. Because of my depression there were times when I felt that Junior didn't want me, that he was closer to Pete, and I felt as if I was holding in my feelings for him, waiting for him to want me. But that's all changed now. He wants my attention and he wants 'mummy cuddles'. Harvey was much calmer around Princess than he was with Junior. He hated it when Junior cried, it would really wind him up, but he's not like that with Princess at all. He kisses her and is gentle with her and calls her his baby sister.

I had so much to be happy about but I couldn't forget the phone call; I couldn't forget hearing Pete say I wasn't his first priority. I tried to carry on as normal, but after a few days I knew I had to do something. So I called Pete when he was out at the doctors with his dad, and, trying not to cry, I told him that, while his parents were staying, I wanted to go to my mum's for a couple of days to give him the time and space to concentrate on his dad. 'I've tried to forget about what you said,' I told him, 'but you really hurt me. Right now I'd rather be at my mum's where I'll be looked after. I know your dad is ill, but I'm your wife and I've just had a baby – we should come first with each other.' Pete insisted that he didn't want me to go, that it would really upset him, and so I agreed to stay. But Pete continued to be stressed and tense. I didn't know how much was down to the situation and how much was because his Meningitis had left him feeling like that. I tried to stay calm, but nothing could have prepared me for the terrible row that was yet to come towards the end of his parents' stay.

* * *

Pete and his parents had just returned one afternoon after yet another visit to the doctors. I was sitting in the kitchen, feeding Princess, and Melodie, my hair-dresser, was halfway through highlighting my hair. As I didn't like Princess being so close to the colour treatment, I asked Pete if he would finish feeding her. So he took her and carried on feeding her. It was lovely watching him with her, but I still worried that he hadn't bonded as well with her as he had with Junior, but I presumed that was probably to do with his dad being ill. A few minutes later he asked me if I had a muslin cloth to wipe her mouth. 'Oh, you can use the baby blanket,' I replied, 'It needs washing and that's what I've been using,' thinking nothing of it. But his mum murmured something to him and Pete asked again if I had a muslin. 'Just use the blanket,' I repeated. But Pete was getting very touchy and said quite aggressively, 'I'm allowed to ask for a muslin, aren't I?'

Here we go, I thought wearily. 'If it makes you feel better, I'll get you one,' I said, and I got up and found one in the laundry room and handed it to him. I decided I'd rather Melodie finished my hair upstairs if Pete was going to be like this. As we left the kitchen, I heard Pete say, 'See what I have to put up with?' which really got my back up and I marched back into the room and said, 'What do you mean? I'm allowed to say what my own daughter's mouth can be wiped with – it's a soft baby blanket, it's not rough.' And he was looking at me as if to say 'Don't even go there!' But I wasn't standing for it and I carried on, 'You were fine a minute ago when you were feeding her and using the blanket and then your mum obviously said something about the blanket being too rough. She's my child; I know what's right for her.' And I turned and walked upstairs, thinking, *God, I don't need a row*. Melodie had barely got started on my hair again when Pete burst into our bedroom. 'How fucking dare you be like that in front of my mum and dad, and make them feel so bad!' he shouted at me.

'Pete!' I exclaimed, 'I've done nothing wrong, I'm not arguing with you.' I was trying to stay calm, knowing how moody his illness had left him and knowing how stressed he was about his dad. He obviously thought I was making a dig at his mum and I suppose, in a way, I was. I was trying to say, 'Don't interfere; don't make me feel like I'm doing something wrong for the baby when I'm not.' Making me feel that I'm not doing the best for my daughter is probably the thing guaranteed to tip me back into depression. 'Are you really going to have an argument about a baby's blanket?' I asked him.

'It was your attitude in front of my mum.' He obviously wasn't going to let this drop.

'I'm the mother! I can say what the hell my baby has her mouth wiped on!' I shouted back. And the row just escalated. Pete was shouting at me that I was ill, that I had to sort my head out, that I had so many issues. All of this in front of Melodie, who was doing her best to defuse the situation by telling Pete that lack of sleep can make people short-tempered. But it was no good. Pete had completely lost it by now, shouting that I had made it obvious that I didn't want his parents to stay at the house, that I hadn't come downstairs to see them, that I hadn't offered them anything, that I had made them feel so unwelcome, and that they were never going to come back to England again because of how I'd made them feel.

'Well, I'm sorry, Pete,' I said, totally shaken by his anger, 'I've just had a baby and I want to be with her, it's nothing to do with your parents.'

Then he walked out. I couldn't believe how angry he had been – it was all so out of proportion. Needing some support, I called my mum and asked her to come over. Pete was out all day. He'd taken his dad to hospital so they could run some tests. But he didn't call to let me know how his dad was or to let me know when he'd be back. I was glad that his dad was finally in hospital, though, and I thought they would at last find out what the matter was with him. I didn't know why Pete had attacked me like that. It was as if things had been building up inside him and he was just looking for any excuse to have a go. I had seen such a different side to him. I thought he was really out of order and I was upset and hurt. I had been so ill with the depression and, although I didn't have it anymore, I still felt vulnerable.

He didn't return until the evening and, when he got back, I was sitting in our bedroom with Princess still feeling shaken by the row, dreading it carrying on, as I know that, if anyone says anything at all about his family, he can't bear it and will stick up for them. But I knew I had done nothing wrong. He marched into the room and, without saying hello to me, said, 'Are you going to feed the baby tonight or am I?'

'I'll feed her,' I replied.

'I want to know when we're each going to look after the kids and when we're not.' He sounded so cold and distant. *What was going on?*

'Why are you saying this?' I asked.

'I've thought about things and I've had enough. I don't want to be with you anymore. This relationship isn't what I thought it would be.'

I was in absolute shock. I just couldn't believe what he was saying.

'Why don't you want to be with me?' I asked, trying to hold it together. And again he said that I had all these problems, that I needed to sort my head out, that he didn't think he could live with me anymore. As heartbreaking as his words were, I was still convinced that he was only saying them because he had been so unwell. I tried to be calm, but then I lost it and I began sobbing. 'Pete, what have I done wrong? I just want to be with you. All I've wanted since I've had the baby is for you to spend time with me and you haven't done that. I understand it's because your dad has been ill, but you've made me feel like shit. But I still want you and I want you to stay. I love you, I don't want you to leave. *Please* don't go.' I paused, wiping away the tears, then, gathering all my strength, I carried on. 'If this is really what you want, I'm going to call a solicitor first thing tomorrow and I'm going to file for divorce.'

'No!' he exclaimed, 'I don't want to divorce you, I just want a separation.'

'No, Pete,' I said firmly, 'You either want to be with me or you don't and, if you don't, then I will divorce you.'

'So you're going to make out that I'm the one who doesn't want to be with you?' he replied, and I said, 'Yes, because I *do* want to be with you, I want to make this relationship work. I'm not having a separation. I'm not having you sleeping with other women behind my back.'

Pete looked at me for a few seconds without saying anything. Then he turned and said he had to go back to the hospital. What had happened to the man I loved? My world felt as if it had fallen apart. I couldn't believe that Pete had said he was leaving me.

Princess woke up for a feed and, as I cradled her in my arms, I thought, *What the hell am I going to do?* I was devastated. I couldn't believe that Pete had said those things to me, couldn't believe that he was leaving me. This was the man I loved more than anything else in the world, the father of my children, the man I thought I would spend the rest of my life with . . . How could this be happening? I think I must have been in shock, but somehow my survival instinct kicked in and I started trying to think about what I should do. The kids are fine, I told myself. Junior is at nursery, Harvey's at school. I know I can financially support all of us. We'll be okay. But even as I thought this, I was crying as I imagined a life without Pete.

My phone beeped, alerting me to a text message. I reached for it straightaway, hoping it would be from Pete saying he was sorry, that he had changed his mind. But it was Mum saying that she was sending Price (what she calls my stepdad) over to have a word with Pete. *Oh no,* I thought, *there's going to be another argument.* But I was so exhausted and distraught from the row that I had no energy to go downstairs and face anyone. I curled up on the bed with Princess beside me and I fell into an exhausted sleep. At some point I woke up and heard voices downstairs. My stepdad, Paul, must have turned up. *I should get up,* I thought, *and see what's going on,* but I was unable to move and I couldn't deal with any more rows. The next thing I remember, Paul was in the room asking me if I was okay. 'Things are going to be all right,' he said and smiled, then left. *Were they?* I thought, it didn't feel like anything was going to be all right ever again . . . Then suddenly Pete walked in.

Oh no, I thought, my heart sinking, *I can't take any more rows.* But he sat down on the bed and said, 'Kate, I'm sorry. I love you and I want us to make another go of our marriage. I realise I haven't been myself and this has got to stop. I do want to be with you. I need you and we are very good for each other.' It was such a relief to hear him say these words, but I still had so many questions.

'So what did you mean when you said you didn't want to be with me anymore?'

'I don't know,' he answered. 'Things have just got too much for me and I know I've said things I shouldn't, but I do want us to work out. I love you, Kate.'

'I love you too, Pete, but I really don't feel that you want to be with me anymore.'

Pete sighed and said, 'I just want us to get on.'

'But Pete,' I replied, 'You're the one who's been

stressing. You seem to think there's been an atmosphere at home with your parents here, but I've been fine about them staying.'

'But you didn't come downstairs and see them,' he replied.

'I just want to bond with the baby and I want you with me; that's all I want. You know how badly I suffered from Postnatal Depression and you being like this really doesn't help. It's lucky that I've got strong again and that I am totally focused on the baby, otherwise the things you've said tonight could have pushed me back into depression.'

'I'm so sorry,' Pete said, then lay next to me on the bed and cuddled me. I think I was still in shock and, even as he held me, I was thinking, *It's going to take a while before I feel that things are back to normal between us,* as I'd been so hurt.

In the morning I told Pete that he really needed to see someone because he seemed so stressed and was so up and down. He promised that he would, but several weeks went by and he still hadn't. He also said he was going to increase the medication he was taking for his panic attacks, but sometimes he would forget to take it at all and it affected his mood, making him anxious and on edge. But overall he seemed much better, less stressed. It helped that his dad was well again by now. He'd finally been diagnosed with an infection and given antibiotics. Once they knew what the problem was and how to treat it, he was soon back to normal, which I was so relieved about.

Sometimes, in the weeks that followed, Pete would be moody with me, but I knew it was the Meningitis that had affected him, so I didn't make a big deal of it. The argument had really hurt me, though, and it took me several weeks to get over it. I thought, *Well then, it's me, Harvey, Junior and Princess and there's no way you're going to take them away from me.* And I'd hated the way he'd tried to make out that I was the one who was ill in the head, when I knew that I wasn't. Pete needed to sort himself out. Things between us were absolutely fine, but there were moments when I didn't feel good about our relationship. When his cousin Miranda came to stay with us, shortly after the row, I confided in her. 'It's made me feel differently about Pete. It's made me think that if he could threaten to leave me over an argument about a baby's blanket then I have to get my barriers back up and be a strong girl again, because inside I've got to prepare myself to be on my own. I can't put up with Pete treating me like that.' But talking to her really helped and, as time went on, I was able to put the argument behind me and move on. And Pete was so loving again, almost back to his old self – we were getting on so well by then that we got through it. As for me, I felt so good that I was determined to lower my medication and, in time, come off it altogether. I felt like the old Kate again. Pete kept saying that I was like the girl he had met in the jungle. Thank God she was back! I think he'd had enough of the moany hormonal cow I'd been, and so had I.

CHAPTER EIGHTEEN

THE GIRL IS BACK

In August we were all due to fly to Cyprus on holiday to stay in Pete's new house and I couldn't wait. I was loving my time off work. I'd been convinced that I would be bored and would be dying to get back, but in fact it was the complete opposite. As I hadn't yet got Princess's passport, we decided that Pete would fly on ahead and get everything ready in the house and I would join him when her passport came through. And we had finally registered her name. We had planned to just call her Princess Tiàamii, but when the registrar asked us if we wanted to include any other names, we suddenly had the idea of having both our nans' names as middle names. So on her birth certificate her name is Princess Tiàamii Crystal Esther Andre. Crystal is after Pete's nan and Esther is after my late nan. With Pete away in Cyprus, it seemed like the perfect opportunity for me to have a girls' night out in London! So I called several of my close friends and we set a date for that Saturday night. Katie Price was going out!

* * *

'Mummy, I want some green chicken!' It was Harvey wandering into my bedroom for about the fifth time when I was trying to get ready for my big night out. I'd only just settled Princess and Pete had Junior with him in Cyprus, otherwise no doubt he'd be wanting something as well. *This isn't how it used to be when I got ready for a night out!* I thought. I'd imagined having the music on loud, trying on lots of different outfits, deciding what to wear, gossiping away with my friends. But the kids kept interrupting me. *Oh well, that's what being a mum of three is like*, I thought, as I quickly put on my make-up. It never takes me long to do my face – I only wear a bit of foundation and blusher, mascara, eyebrow pencil and lip gloss. I couldn't wear the revealing clothes that I wanted to, as I'd only had Princess six weeks ago, so I had to cover up my cleavage and stomach. My legs were all I had out on display in a bright yellow mini dress.

The evening started to liven up when we all piled into the car and were driven to London. We cracked open the champagne and sang along raucously to eighties hits – *This is more like it!* I thought. Before going to the club we dropped by at the Sanderson, a chic hotel with a glamorous bar that serves wicked strawberry daiquiris – I love them! But they knock your head off. I didn't even have to pay for the drinks, as some guy sitting at the bar offered to pick up the bill. I'm not saying he'll read this book, but if he does, thanks! I was with my friends Jamelia, Michelle, Julie and Jo and a couple of journalists from *OK!* Marcia and Emma, joined us too, as I know them really well. I was cool about hanging out with them, because it wasn't as if I was going to be getting up to anything ... I also had a security guy with me, as the paps can get a bit mad around the car. Nicola, from my management, was with us all too. She had said she wasn't going to come, but I discovered that my mum had phoned her and told her to make sure that someone from my management went with me. God knows what Mum thought I was going to get up to . . . When I saw Mum the next day, I said, 'Why are you getting involved? I'm twenty-nine years of age. If I want to go out and have a few drinks, I will!' It wasn't exactly a normal night out for me, though, with all those eyeballs watching me, making sure I didn't do anything. It was all 'Don't do this, don't do that!' And I thought, *Do they expect me to just stand there and not look at anyone or say anything?!*

From the Sanderson we went to Mo*vida – a fantastic club near Oxford Street. The champagne was flowing and I was in my own little world, dancing non-stop and drinking. I was loving being out! This was just what I needed. At one point I saw one of my exes, the pop singer Gareth Gates – we'd had a brief secret relationship in 2002. I had really liked him and felt very let down when he ended it. It was at a time when I felt particularly vulnerable because I was pregnant with Harvey and was facing life as a single parent. Gareth was paranoid about the press finding out about us and what that might do to his music career. And when the press finally did get hold of the story, he denied that he'd ever had a relationship with me. He said some pretty hurtful things as well. He said that I was lying, and he even said, 'As if it would be Jordan when there are so many other lovely girls out there.' A year later, though, he finally admitted that we'd had an affair and, in 2006, he said that he regretted lying about it. When I saw him, I just briefly said hi. I'm so over what happened between us. It's history. I was more interested in dancing. I kept going over to the DJ and asking him to play this one song, 'Wifey', by Next. I think he agreed to play it once, which I should be grateful for, as it's a club for everyone and not supposed to cater for just Katie Price's tastes!

Before we went out that night I was giving it large to all my friends, saying, 'We'll be home at five or six in the morning!' But in the end I only lasted an hour in the club. I'm such a light-weight with alcohol now that, by quarter past one, I just wanted to go home and get into bed! The tabloid and celeb magazines coverage of my night out made me laugh – they all talked about how Jordan the party animal was back. They also made a big deal about the fact that I wasn't wearing my wedding ring, speculating whether our marriage was in crisis, when the truth was it was in the safe at home which I didn't know how to open because it has a really complicated lock! I phoned Pete the next day to tell him all about my night, mentioning that I had seen Gareth Gates and that I'd said hello because I wanted Pete to hear about it from me, not read about it in the press, where they'd be trying to make it into something it wasn't. And he wasn't furious about my drunken night – as it was made to look, splashed over one magazine – he was just pleased that I'd had a good time. I was a bit hungover, though, and looking after a baby when you've got a headache is not to be recommended . . . But I'd got my night-out itch out of my system and I didn't think I'd be going clubbing again for a while.

But, a few days later, Lipsy, the clothing company who have lent me clothes for years, invited me to their party at Jewel, a really cool bar in the West End. I decided it would be a laugh to go and invited my friend Michelle Scott-Heaton along. I had a great time and this time I paced my drinking so the night lasted

quite a bit longer. After the party we hit several clubs
with my friends Gary and Phil, including Funky
Buddha and Aura in Mayfair, ending up at Balans in
Soho, where I finished the night with a chicken Thai
curry, which is what I always have when I go there.
And no way was I as drunk as I had been on my first
night out. But the tabloids went mental, printing
stories that I'd thrown up in the loos and that I'd
come out with some outrageous comments. And do
you know what? It was all bollocks! And if the worst
thing they can say is that I was drunk, well so what?
All I'd done was dance, have a laugh, have a few
drinks and just let my hair down – mission accom-
plished. But it was nothing like my old clubbing
days, which, I admit, were wild . . . To be honest, I'm
not even bothered about clubbing anymore. Just,
once in a while, I'd like to stir the pot.

* * *

'Blue rectangle swimming pool, Mummy,' Harvey
said, for about the twentieth time that morning. He
was happily swimming round the pool at the holiday
house in Cyprus.

'Yes, Harvey,' I replied, knowing that if I didn't he

would get upset. I was lying by the pool trying to relax and sunbathe, but with three kids there was not much chance of that! But I didn't mind. They were all so happy and that's what mattered, and I was so happy as well. I'd flown over with Harvey and Princess the day before. Let me tell you that trying to manage a wheelchair and a buggy as well as our luggage and two kids at an airport is not easy. I had to ask for a lot of assistance. Before that, I had to tackle the packing and, because Harvey wasn't yet toilet trained, it was like having three babies. I had to pack large nappies for him, medium nappies for Junior and small ones for Princess, as well as their toys, their blankets and their clothes. As we travelled to Cyprus, I had to explain absolutely everything to Harvey so he wouldn't get upset. On the plane he was pretty good, as he liked opening and closing the window blind, which probably wound everyone up, but at least he was happy. At one point I had to change his nappy and the only space I could do it was where the cabin crew stand; and I had to get someone to hold Princess while I did. Ah, I do lead a glamorous life! But any stress just went away when I met up with Pete and Junior again. I'd really missed them. I absolutely loved the new house – it's ultra modern and has such a great feeling of space and I immediately felt at home.

We had such a brilliant holiday. Pete and me didn't argue once. In the past, whenever we went to Cyprus, we would always end up having a massive row, but not this time. His parents were staying nearby and we all got on fine. In fact, on a couple of occasions I let his mum look after Princess for a few hours and I didn't feel anything negative about it like I had done in the past – I was just happy to let her have time with her granddaughter. It was great seeing the kids enjoying themselves. Harvey was so easy to look after at the holiday house; in fact, he was easier than he is at home. All he wanted to do was swim in the pool and talk about the blue rectangle swimming pool! Pete's forever doing impressions and one of his favourite is of Dr Evil from the Austin Powers movies, he's even got a mini Dr Evil doll and he would throw it into the pool and the boys would have to swim and get it. Harvey loved the game and was constantly saying, 'I want Dr Elvin,' (as he calls him) in the 'blue rectangle swimming pool'. Once Harvey finds something he likes, he's happy to do it all the time, whereas Junior needs more stimulation and attention. As for Princess, she is such a contented baby.

Halfway through the holiday I had to fly home for a couple of days because it was the launch of my new perfume – Stunning. I found it really hard to leave Princess behind with Pete. When he dropped me off at the airport I almost wanted to beg him to let me take her with me! It would have been hard, though, as I had a full day's work ahead of me, and, if she cries, I'm the only one who can settle her, or at least I feel I am. I hadn't been parted from her at all and I had taken her with me everywhere I went. But I also thought it would be good for Pete to look after her. 'Oh my God,' was his first reaction when I told him he should. 'Do you think I'll be okay with her?'

'Pete, you know how to look after a baby!' I replied. 'And it would be good for you to have some time with her, instead of me hogging her!'

I'd wanted to have my own perfume for ages. I've always been a big fan of perfume, as I think it's important for a girl to smell nice. I made all the decisions from choosing the scent, to designing the bottle and box. I loved the result and it really reflected me – a gorgeous-smelling pink perfume in a jewel shaped bottle with crystals decorating the lid – not that I'm saying I'm gorgeous! I'd chosen the fragrance from hundreds of perfumes and I'd had to make the short list when I was pregnant. This wasn't an ideal time to be choosing scents, because when you're pregnant your sense of smell is much more sensitive, so it was agreed that I would make my final choice when I'd had the baby and when my sense of smell was back to normal. I smelled my way through some gorgeous ones and some vile ones! In the end I chose three, with one as my particular favourite. In fact, after I'd had the baby it turned out I still chose my original favourite. It's a floral and feminine fragrance, strong with hints of jasmine and mandarin – sorry to sound a bit poncey, but it's not easy describing perfumes! Take it from me, it smells stunning!

I'd also chosen the picture for the box. I'd done the shoot in America with the renowned photographer Richard McLaren, who also shot the cover of this book. He's photographed so many stars, from Halle Berry to Pamela Anderson, and I absolutely love his pictures. I was actually quite heavily pregnant when

the picture was taken for the perfume, but you can't
see as it's a head shot. I wanted the look to be really
American, a kind of Barbie look, which I've
definitely got with my long platinum blonde hair and
my tanned skin and the bling of my wedding ring. Of
course I wanted something out of the ordinary for
the launch. I had the idea of wearing something
spectacular and rotating slowly like a figure on top of
a huge jewellery box. I was desperate to wear something skimpy again, as I was so sick of wearing big
frumpy dresses! But then I thought, if I wear a bikini,
it won't have the right look, as it won't necessarily be
beautiful, and that's the look I need, so I went for a
full-length pale pink satin ball gown by one of my
favourite designers, Hollywood Dreams.

The launch was held at Kensington Roof Gardens
in West London. It was the first work I'd done since
having the baby and I really wanted it to go well.
Loads of press turned up and I made sure I had my
wedding ring on and I held it up so that everyone
could see. It was a full-on day, so it was just as well
that I didn't have Princess with me, though I missed
her very much and couldn't wait to see her again.
Claire had her baby son with her and the press took

pictures of him thinking it was Princess. My perfume went to number one and rapidly sold out in some stores, which I was thrilled about, but I actually didn't feel as though I was in competition with anyone, as there are so many perfumes on the market.

Emotionally, I felt in such a good place, a million miles from where I'd been when I had Postnatal Depression. I can't tell you how wonderful it was to feel like my old self again – strong, confident, happy and sexy. Yes! At last I felt like making love with Pete again and it was brilliant, because our sex life has certainly had its ups and downs over the last couple of years – downs mainly . . . It was crap when I was pregnant with Junior and when I suffered from Postnatal Depression, then it perked up briefly, long enough for me to get pregnant again. But then came the terrible morning sickness and the tragic mis-carriage. Then I became pregnant again, but with that came yet more morning sickness. Harvey had his horrific accident, and then, just as he was getting better, Pete was struck down with Meningitis – none of which was likely to put either one of us in the mood. By the time he recovered, I was so heavily pregnant I could hardly move, so during this time sex was hardly the first thing on my mind! But time has gone by so quickly that we haven't had time to worry about the lack of sex and it hasn't even been an issue between us. I think you know when you've met your right partner when your relationship isn't just based on sex. Before I met Pete I loved sex and so did he, and I'm not saying we don't love it anymore, because of course we do, but we've had so much to deal with. Our desire for each other is still strong and now our sex life is back to normal – letting our imagination run wild and making up for all the time we've missed . . . I'm sure I'll share my secrets in the next book.

Towards the end of my pregnancy with Princess we both kept saying that we couldn't wait for me not to be pregnant, for my hormones to be back to normal so that we could just enjoy life. We've done everything back to front, you see – we had Junior, then got married – and everything has happened so quickly. Now I really feel we can start our honeymoon period and just enjoy our life together with no stress. We have our family, our careers are going well and our marriage is stronger than ever before. I can't see what can go wrong now after all we've been through. I guess there's always something, but I really hope not, as we've had more than our fair share of traumas.

I definitely think having a third child has evened out things in our family. Before Princess was born, Pete often thought I gave Harvey more attention than Junior, but that's changed now. When he watched me with the baby, Pete kept saying he couldn't believe how different I was with her and how close I was to her. And that filled me with both happiness and a little sadness because those early months of Junior's life are such a blur. I think it makes Pete and all the people I'm close to realise just how ill I was with depression. But that's behind me now and I really want to focus on all the positive things in my life. Pete is happy because now I've got two children by him and, although he never separates Harvey and Junior, he's obviously going to have a different bond with his own children. Now that I've got my boys and my little girl, we do feel more complete as a family. I haven't finished yet, though! I still want more kids – possibly another three. But not for a couple of years at least, because my body needs a rest. However, we'll have to wait and see, because I know what I'm like and as soon as I'd had Princess I wanted another one.

So what does the future hold? We're definitely going to renew our vows in 2008. There was a time when things weren't good between us, and Pete even said that he didn't know if he wanted to renew them, that we should just see what happens. But we're through that now and he wants to as much as I do. We want an event as big as our wedding, just as fairy-tale-like, but maybe not quite so pink. I've even promised Pete that I will take on his surname. I know it seems soon to renew them after just three years, but, as a couple, we've already been through what most people experience in a lifetime. It would be a celebration of our love and a new start.

Next year I'm thirty and I'm planning a massive party. I've got more novels coming out, more TV series, more trips to America and more merchandise, so I will be busy, but I love it! I'm planning to learn dressage. I'll probably go brunette, then blonde, brunette, and blonde again a few times; and I can guarantee I'll be having more wild nights out with the girls! By the time this book is out, I should also finally have had my boobs done again. This time it's going to happen! They need some serious tweaking . . . Once they're done, Jordan will be back. And I am sure there will be so many more things happening – as I've said before, never underestimate *the Pricey*.

There's so much to look forward to, but I know it wouldn't mean a thing if I didn't have my family. They give my life meaning.